The Science Explorer

**Family Experiments
from the World's
Favorite Hands-On
Science Museum**

Pat Murphy, Ellen Klages, Linda Shore,
and the Staff of the Exploratorium

Illustrated by Jason Gorski

An Owl Book   **Henry Holt and Company**   **New York**

Henry Holt and Company, Inc.
Publishers since 1866
115 West 18th Street
New York, New York 10011

Henry Holt® is a registered trademark of
Henry Holt and Company, Inc.

Published in Canada by Fitzhenry & Whiteside Ltd.,
195 Allstate Parkway, Markham, Ontario L3R 4T8.

Library of Congress Cataloging-in-Publication Data
The science explorer: the best family activities and experiments from
the world's favorite hands-on science museum / Pat Murphy . . .
[et al.].
    p.   cm.—(An Exploratorium science-at-home book)
    "An Owl book."
    Includes index.
    1. Science—Experiments. 2. Science—Experiments—Juvenile
literature. 3. Scientific recreations. 4. Science museums—Educa-
tional aspects. I. Murphy, Pat. II. Series.
Q182.3.S335   1996
507.8—dc20

96-16847
CIP

ISBN 0-8050-4536-8 (An Owl Book: pbk.)

Henry Holt books are available for special promotions and premiums.
For details contact: Director, Special Markets.

First Edition—1996

Designed by Kate Nichols and Kelly Soong

Printed in the United States of America
All first editions are printed on acid-free paper. ∞

10 9 8 7 6 5 4 3 2 1

Be careful! The experiments in this publication were designed with safety and success in mind. But even the simplest activity or the most common materials can be harmful when mishandled or misused.

Exploratorium® is a registered trademark and service mark of The Exploratorium.

This material is based on work supported by the National Science Foundation under Grant No. ESI-9355630. Opinions expressed are those of the authors and not necessarily those of the foundation.

This project was funded, in part, by a generous gift from the Pacific Telesis Foundation.

7UP® is a registered trademark of The Seven-Up Company.
Alka-Seltzer® is a registered trademark of Bayer Corporation.
Ultra Dawn® is a registered trademark of Procter & Gamble.
X-Acto® is a registered trademark of Hunt Manufacturing Co.
Styrofoam® is a registered trademark of Dow Chemical Company.
Saran Wrap® is a registered trademark of DowBrands.
Xerox® is a registered trademark of Xerox Corporation.
Plexiglas® is a registered trademark of Rohm and Haas Company.
M&M's® is a registered trademark of Mars, Inc.
Silly Putty® is a registered trademark of Binney & Smith Inc., used with permission.
Boraxo® is a registered trademark of The Dial Corporation.
Play-Doh® is a registered trademark of Tonka Corporation.

Illustrations of the bird/antelope illusion on page 50 are from *Patterns of Discovery,* by N. R. Hansen. Copyright 1958 Cambridge University Press. Reprinted with permission of Cambridge University Press.

For all the families

who eagerly and enthusiastically

tested these experiments,

and for all the folks—on the Exploratorium staff

and elsewhere—who helped create

these experiments

Contents

Having Fun with Science

An Introduction for Parents

This book is for curious kids and for grown-ups who want to encourage a child's invention, curiosity, and eagerness to explore—while having fun. It's filled with science activities that are fun to do and require little or no preparation.

These experiments were developed at the Exploratorium, San Francisco's hands-on museum of science, art, and human perception. All of them have been tested by hundreds of families in their own homes, and all of them can be done with simple materials from your local grocery store or drugstore.

The Exploratorium's Science-at-Home team wrote this book for people who may not know anything about science—but want to explore the world around them. You don't need to know about science to have a great time blowing bubbles, making musical instruments and flying toys, creating shimmering colors and startling sparks, and finding the wonder in everyday things. And if doing these things makes you curious, you'll find straightforward explanations that will answer your questions about what's going on in each experiment.

Science is a way of looking at the world, a way of experimenting to figure out how things work. You may discover, as you fool around with bubbles and colors and sound and light, that you know more about science than you thought.

Have fun!

This is the Science-at-Home team, making Straw Oboes. From left to right: Ellen Klages, Pat Murphy, and Linda Shore

Illustrator Jason Gorski, an essential part of the Science-At-Home team, is represented here by some of the characters he created for this book. Clockwise from upper left: Carmen, Tina, Jesse, Russell, Violet, Joey, and Rachel.

How to Use This Book

The Science Explorer is designed for kids and grown-ups to use, separately and together. Some experiments are labeled "Kids Can Do It!" This means kids can read and do these experiments with little or no grown-up supervision.

In each chapter, one or two experiments are labeled "Exploring Together." These give grown-ups a chance to experiment along with kids, encouraging kids to ask questions (and maybe ask a few questions themselves). Kids may need a little help with the experiments labeled "Exploring Together." Some of these experiments are a little tricky, and some involve using a sharp tool or another object that could be dangerous.

When your family starts experimenting, don't be surprised if grown-ups want to try some of the experiments that are labeled "Kids Can Do It!" In the families that tested these activities, grown-ups found themselves playing with Outrageous Ooze (page 112) after the kids had gone to bed, showing their Hoopsters (page 62) to their friends, and generally having a great time experimenting with science.

Explanations Are Optional

In addition, this book includes explanations that grown-ups can use to answer questions that may come up while the kids are experimenting. These explanations are in boxes labeled "What's Going On?" They are written for grown-ups who have no scientific background.

We suggest that grown-ups read these explanations and share them with the kids—if they ask. But the kids may not ask. Some kids want explanations, but many others are just interested in playing around and experimenting. Rather than trying to explain, we advise grown-ups to encourage a child's natural tendency to figure out what will happen when he or she changes an experiment. Will a balloon make pepper jump higher than a plastic spoon? (See page 66.) Try it! You can find your own answer by experimenting.

You Can Make Your Own Discoveries

The instructions in this book can help you start experimenting. But your explorations don't have to end when you read the last instruction. This book is just the beginning.

If you like to cook (or like to eat), you probably know that there are different types of cooks. There are cooks who follow a recipe exactly, never changing a thing. And then there are cooks who like to change a little something every time and taste-test the results.

You can approach our instructions in the same way that a creative cook approaches a recipe. Change a little something and see what happens.

We've suggested some changes to try—but our suggestions are just the beginning. What other modifications can you and your kids come up with? Your Spinning Blimp (page 52) flies all right—but maybe a blimp with a longer tail would spin even better. Maybe you've made a successful Bubble Bomb (page 2) with a sandwich bag. Can you make one with a bigger bag?

While you're experimenting, it may look like you're just fooling around. You're not following any instructions; you're trying a little of this and a little of that. This approach to the world is at the heart of the scientific process. Many scientific discoveries (and some fabulous recipes) have come about because someone was "just fooling around."

An important part of fooling around is accepting that everything you try isn't going to be a success. Maybe your Spinning Blimp takes a nosedive or your giant Bubble Bomb is a dud. That's okay—in fact, that's great. You've learned something about what doesn't work, which is an important bit of information. And maybe sometime you'll *want* to make a blimp that dives—and you'll know how. This is what being a "science explorer" is all about!

Let Us Know What You Think!

Finally, if you're being scientific, then part of fooling around is keeping track of your results and sharing them with others. What works well? What doesn't work at all? If you come up with a new experiment (or a modification of an old one) that you think is fun, let us know. We'd like to try it too.

You can contact us at:

The Science Explorer
Henry Holt and Company
115 West 18th Street
New York, NY 10011

Or you can send us E-mail at:

home_science@exploratorium.edu

What Should I Try First?

This book has experiments and activities that are fun in a variety of situations. Use these lists to help you choose an activity that fits the time you have and what you're doing—whether you want to have fun at a family picnic on a sunny day or you need a quiet activity for a rainy afternoon. To help you plan ahead, we've also listed experiments that require some advance preparation.

How Long Will It Take?

Maybe you have just a few minutes to spare—or a rainy afternoon that seems endless. We've marked each experiment with a clock that indicates about how much time it will take. This is based on our best estimate of the shortest time needed to do the experiment. If an experiment intrigues you, you may find yourself spending more time—or returning to the experiment later.

 means 15 minutes or less

 means 15 minutes to 1 hour

 means 1 hour or more

Some experiments are quick and intriguing. Trying these often leads kids (and grown-ups) to try the other experiments in the same chapter. These are our favorite quick experiments:

Reflecting Rainbows (page 18)
Floaters (page 38)
Hot Dog Finger (page 39)
Spinning Blimps (page 52)
Jumping Pepper (page 66)
Straw Oboe (page 74)
Head Harp (page 93)

Will It Work with a Group?

Maybe you have an entire birthday party or scout troop to entertain. These experiments work well with groups:

Bubble Bomb (page 2)
Bubble Blimps (page 6)
Bubble Prints (page 10)
My Face Is a Vase! (page 48)
Spinning Blimps (page 52)
Roto-Copter (page 54)
Straw Oboe (page 74)
Rain Sticks (page 76)
The Tingler (page 78)
Cups of Mystery (page 98)
ExploraGoo (page 108)
Outrageous Ooze (page 112)

Where Can I Do It?

Maybe it's a sunny day and you want to play outside. Here are some experiments that are best done outdoors:

Bubble Bomb (page 2)
Bubble Blimps (page 6)
Rainbows on Your Lawn (page 16)
Fabulous Foam Flyer (The F-3) (page 58)
Hoopster (page 62)
Sound Safari (page 90)

Or maybe it's raining out, and you're trapped inside with a bored kid. Here are some quiet, indoor experiments:

Or maybe you just want to get the kids into the bathtub. Here are two activities that are great in the bath:

What If I Want to Do Something That's More Artistic?

Maybe you've got kids who love art but aren't so sure about science.

Here are some experiments that may spark their curiosity:

Which Experiments Require Advance Planning?

There's nothing worse than being all ready to do an experiment—and discovering you don't have all the stuff you need.

Some experiments are easier if you have photocopies. If you want to be prepared, we suggest photocopying these pages:

Some experiments require materials that you may have to accumulate or make a special trip to the store to get. Here's the list of those experiments. Check the page to see exactly what you need:

A NOTE ON GRAMMAR

The Science-at-Home team is dedicated to encouraging both girls and boys to experiment and explore their world. We are concerned that subtle cultural biases tend to discourage girls from pursuing an interest in science.

With that in mind, we found ourselves in a dilemma. We did not want to use only "he" or only "she" to refer to an unspecified friend or helper. But we also didn't want to invent a new pronoun or resort to grammatical errors like "Have your friend hold the cup to their ear." Our solution was to use "she" sometimes and "he" sometimes—so that some of your helpers are girls and some are boys.

Are You a Science Explorer?

You're probably already a scientist and don't even know it. Scientists are people who are curious about the world and the things in it. They like to look at how things work or how they change. They like to explore and try out new ideas. They like to make messes, ask questions, and fool around.

This book is full of fun ways to experiment with science, using ordinary stuff you have around the house.

Your Instant Science Lab Box

When the Science-at-Home team first started experimenting, we kept having to stop and look for the scissors or a balloon or a pen that worked. Finally we got a cardboard box and filled it with the things we used all the time. It might look like a box full of junk to some people, but we call it the Instant Science Lab Box.

To make your own Instant Science Lab Box, all you need is a big cardboard box and the things on this list.

You'll use these things for a lot of experiments. If something has this mark (•) it means you'll need to plan ahead to save this usually recycled stuff.

big cardboard box
aluminum pie pan
a package of balloons
• soda bottle (empty)

- soda can (empty)
- cardboard tube (from a roll of paper towels or wrapping paper)
- clear plastic lid (from yogurt or margarine)
pad of construction paper
- corrugated cardboard
a few cotton swabs
a package of file cards
flashlight
- jar with a lid
markers (black and colored ones)
- newspaper
paper (notebook size)
a few paperclips
pencil
a few pipe cleaners
a handful of plastic straws
a few pushpins or thumbtacks
a handful of rubber bands
ruler
scissors
a spoon
string
tape (clear plastic tape and masking tape)
a few toothpicks
white glue
wire coat hangers
- two yogurt containers (empty)

Things to Borrow from Your Kitchen

For some experiments you'll need things from your family's kitchen. *Don't* keep these things in your Instant Science Lab Box. Just ask if you can borrow these things for a while, then put them back when you're done.

aluminum foil
baking soda
beans (dry)
bowl
bucket
butter knife (not a sharp knife)
can of soda (full)
can opener
carrot
coffee cup
coffee filter
cookie cutters
cookie sheet
cornstarch
cup or mug
dish soap
flat baking dish
food coloring
funnel
lid from a pot or pan
marshmallows
measuring cup
measuring spoons
milk
paper towels
pepper
plastic bags (zipper-type), sandwich size
plastic wrap
raisins
rice
salt
spoon
vinegar
wooden spoon

Ask a Grown-up for These Things

For some experiments, you'll need tools and equipment or furniture that you'll have to ask a grown-up to get for you. You'll probably want a grown-up to help you with these experiments, too.

chair
compact disc (CD)
duct tape (or packing tape)
lamp
magnifying glass
microwave oven
nails
rubbing alcohol
screwdriver
• tin cans (3 of each size; see page 82)
towel
TV
utility knife or X-Acto knife
VCR

Things to Get at a Store

For just a few experiments, you'll need things that your family may not keep around the house. Ask a grown-up to get these things from a store.

Borax laundry product (or Boraxo hand soap)
clear nail polish
disposable camera (from a camera store; see page 26)
jar of red pickled cabbage
Pringles potato chips can
• Styrofoam trays from the supermarket

That's it! That's everything you need to be a scientist, right at home. With what's on these lists, you can to do any experiment in this book, anytime you want.

So what are you waiting for?

1 BLOWING, BOUNCING, BURSTING BUBBLES

In 1983, the Exploratorium held its first Bubble Festival. People came from all over the United States to show us their amazing bubbles. They showed us cubical bubbles and bubble caterpillars, bubble towers and giant bubbles, bubbles that burst in less than a minute and bubbles that could sit on a shelf for almost a year.

Some people think studying bubbles is silly. At the Exploratorium, we disagree— and we know plenty of scientists, artists, teachers, and experimenters who are on our side.

Take, for example, Tom Noddy, a traveling bubble performer who spent months figuring out how to blow a bubble in the shape of a cube. Or consider Eiffel Plasterer, a high school teacher who discovered that bubbles provided a great way to teach students about science. Or Eugene Tsui, an architect who studied bubbles to figure out how to build the most efficient building. One scientist, Donald Glaser, a nuclear physicist, even won the Nobel Prize for inventing the bubble chamber. In this device, tiny bubbles reveal something that scientists couldn't see any other way—the paths followed by particles that are smaller than an atom. All these people played with bubbles—and at the same time took them very seriously.

This is Eiffel Plasterer, also known as Mr. Bubbles, at one of his "Bubbles Concertos" in 1948. A high school teacher in Huntington, Indiana, Eiffel used bubbles to teach his students about science. He experimented with long-lasting soap bubbles and blew one bubble that he kept in a jar on his shelf for a record 340 days.

You can blow bubbles bigger than your dog, pop a plastic bag with the power of fizz, and make your own light show with amazing bubble colors!

Bubble Bomb

Using baking soda and vinegar, you can pop a plastic bag with the power of fizz.

Making a Bubble Bomb can be tricky. Get a grown-up to help.

What Do I Need?

- water
- measuring cup
- zipper-lock plastic sandwich bags
- paper towel
- tablespoon
- baking soda
- vinegar

What Do I Do?

1 Figure out where you want to explode your Bubble Bomb. Sometimes the bags make a mess when they pop, so you may want to experiment outside. If it's a rainy day, you can explode your Bubble Bombs in the bathtub or sink.

2 It's very important to use a bag without holes. To test the zipper-lock bag, put about half a cup of water into it. Zip it closed and turn it upside down. If no water leaks out, you can use that bag. Unzip it and pour out the water. If the bag leaks, try another one. Keep testing bags until you find one that doesn't leak.

3 Tear a paper towel into a square that measures about 5 inches by 5 inches. Put 1½ tablespoons of baking soda in the center of the square, then fold the square as shown in the picture, with the baking soda inside. This is your "time-release packet."

4 Pour into your plastic bag:

  ¼ cup of warm water
  ½ cup of vinegar

5 Now here's the tricky part. You need to drop the time-release packet into the vinegar and zip the bag closed *before* the fizzing gets out of control.

You can zip the bag halfway closed, then stuff the packet in and zip the bag closed the rest of the way in a hurry. Or you can put the time-release packet into the mouth of the bag and hold it up out of the vinegar by pinching the sides of the bag. Zip the bag closed and then let the packet drop into the vinegar.

One way or another, get the packet in the vinegar and zip the bag closed.

6 Shake the bag a little, put it in the sink or on the ground, and stand back! The bag will puff up dramatically and pop with a bang.

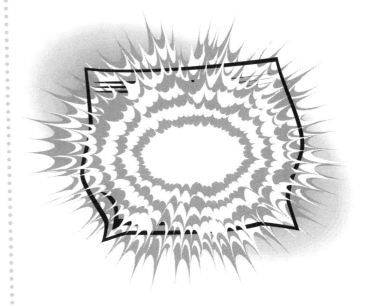

What's Going On?

Why does the Bubble Bomb explode?

The bubbles in the Bubble Bomb are filled with carbon dioxide, a gas that forms when the vinegar (an acid) reacts with the baking soda (a base).

If you've ever made a cake or baked a loaf of quick bread (the kind that doesn't use yeast), you've already done some experimenting with the bubbles that come from an acid-base reaction. Most cakes and quick breads rise because of bubbles in their batter. Those bubbles, like the ones in your Bubble Bomb, are created by the chemical reaction of an acid and a base.

Take a look at a recipe for quick bread. If the recipe includes baking soda but no baking powder, it will probably also include an ingredient that's acidic—such as buttermilk, sour milk, or orange juice.

Quick-bread recipes may call for baking powder in addition to or instead of baking soda. Baking powder is made by combining baking soda with an acidic ingredient, such as tartaric acid or calcium acid phosphate. When you add water to baking powder, it will fizz as the acid and base interact. In fact, if you ever run out of baking powder, you can make your own by mixing two teaspoons cream of tartar (it provides the acid), one teaspoon of baking soda (it's the base), and a half-teaspoon of salt.

Balloon Blowup

Not all bubbles are made with soap!

What Do I Need?

- vinegar
- water
- bottle with a narrow neck
- funnel or a straw
- balloon (any size or shape will work)
- baking soda

What Do I Do?

1 Pour about an inch of liquid—half vinegar, half water—into the bottle.

2 Use the funnel to fill the balloon half full of baking soda. (If you don't have a funnel, you can use a straw to load the balloon. Stick the straw into the baking soda, and put your finger over the top of the straw. Lift the straw out, put it into the balloon, and blow into or tap the straw gently.)

3 Stretch the end of the balloon over the neck of the bottle. Make sure it's on tight! Be sure the rest of the balloon dangles down next to the bottle, so no baking soda gets into the bottle yet.

4 Hold the balloon at the bottle's neck, and then lift up the rest of the balloon straight up so that all the baking soda falls into the liquid in the bottle.

5 Wow! Hear the fizz? There are thousands of bubbles! And look what's happening to the balloon. . . .

4

Raisin City Music Hall

For more bubble fun you'll need:

- can of clear soda (like ginger ale, lemon-lime soda, or club soda)
- raisins
- a glass

Pour the soda into a glass. Drop in five or six small raisins. If you have big raisins, ask a grown-up to cut them in half or in quarters and then drop them into the soda. Watch tiny bubbles form all over the raisins. In a minute or so, they will start to wiggle around and dance. Then they'll float up to the top of the soda. After a minute, they'll sink back down again. If you tap on the side of the glass, they'll sink right away. How long will they keep dancing?

Wow! I Didn't Know That!

Fizzy liquids get into your intestines faster than other liquids. The bubbles in soda or Alka-Seltzer tickle the exit valve in your stomach, and it opens.

What's Going On?

Why does the balloon inflate?

Like the bubbles in the Bubble Bomb (page 2), these bubbles form when vinegar (an acid) reacts with the baking soda (a base). This reaction produces carbon dioxide gas, which bubbles out of the liquid and fills the balloon.

Carbon dioxide is the same gas that makes soda pop bubbly. When you open a can of soda, carbon dioxide bubbles out of the liquid and your soda fizzes.

How do those bubbles get into the soda in the first place and why do they bubble out when you open the can or bottle? Two conditions determine how much carbon dioxide can dissolve in a liquid: temperature and pressure. More gas will dissolve in a cold liquid that's under high pressure than in a warm liquid that's not under pressure.

Soda manufacturers inject cold liquid with pressurized carbon dioxide, then bottle the drink under high pressure. A refrigerated can of 7UP® has an internal pressure of about 30 pounds per square inch. When you open the can, you release the pressure. Atmospheric pressure is only about 14 pounds per square inch. With this sudden drop in pressure, the carbon dioxide comes bubbling out of the soda.

The bubbles in these bubbly beverages don't just tickle your tongue—they change the flavor of what you're drinking. The carbon dioxide in the soda forms carbonic acid, which offsets the sweet taste of the drink. That's why soda (or champagne) that's flat tastes sweeter than it does when it's still bubbly.

Bubble Blimps

Go outside and blow a bubble bigger than your dog!

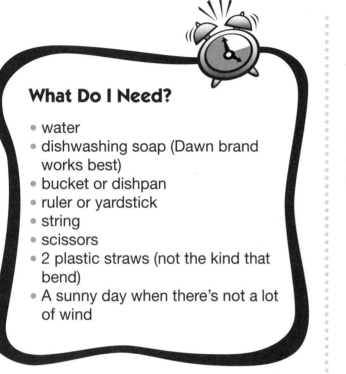

What Do I Need?

- water
- dishwashing soap (Dawn brand works best)
- bucket or dishpan
- ruler or yardstick
- string
- scissors
- 2 plastic straws (not the kind that bend)
- A sunny day when there's not a lot of wind

What Do I Do?

1 Mix up a gallon of the bubble juice. (Don't drink it. Yuck!)

Bubble Juice

1 gallon water
⅔ cup dishwashing soap

Mix all the ingredients together in a big bucket or dishpan. If you make your bubble juice the day before you want to use it, you'll get bigger, stronger bubbles, but it's pretty good right away, too.

---

2 Cut a piece of string about 3 feet long. Thread it through two plastic straws. Tie the ends of the string together.

3 Hold one straw in each hand and pull until you make a rectangle with a straw at each end. Now you have a String-ola!

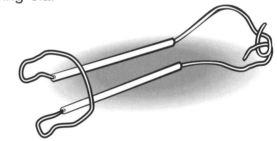

4 Take your bucket of bubble juice and your String-ola outside. (A day that's not too windy is best.)

5 Dip your String-ola (and your hands) all the way into the bubble juice. Hold the straws together and lift them out. When your String-ola is all the way out of the bubble juice, pull your hands apart—s-l-o-w-l-y. Check to make sure there's a soap film between the straws. If not, dip your String-ola in the bucket and try again.

6 Hold your String-ola out in front of you. Walk backward to move your String-ola through the air. You'll make a really, really big bubble bulge.

7 When you think the bubble bulge is big enough, put your hands together until the straws touch again. When the straws touch, the bubble can float off by itself. With a little practice, you can turn a bubble bulge into a huge bubble.

Wow! I Didn't Know That!

Bubble gum was invented by Walter Diemer, an employee of the Fleer Company, in 1928. The gum was named Dubble Bubble. It was pink because that was the only color food coloring Diemer had when he made the first successful batch.

What's Going On?

Why are small bubbles round? Why aren't the Bubble Blimps round?

A soap bubble is a thin film of soap and water stretched around a puff of air. The soap film is elastic. When you blow against a soap film on a bubble wand, it stretches. When a bubble breaks free, the soap film contracts to make the smallest possible surface that can contain the puff of air.

That's why most small, free-floating bubbles are spherical. A sphere is the shape that provides the most space for the air with the least stretching of the soap film. This shape has the most volume with the least surface area.

If you blow some Bubble Blimps, you'll notice that they billow and shift their shape. Each passing breeze pushes on the soap film, stretching it so that the bubble wiggles this way and that. These giant bubbles almost always pop before they stabilize to form a sphere.

A free-floating soap bubble is round for the same reason that a cat curls into a ball on a cold night. That's the shape that offers the largest volume with the smallest surface area. The cat minimizes its surface area to keep warm—the less surface the cat exposes to the air, the less heat the animal loses.

Building with Bubbles

You can make piles, domes, and wiggly lines of bubbles.

What Do I Need?

- bubble juice (see recipe on page 6)
- cookie sheet with sides (or a flat baking dish)
- plastic straw
- cup of water

What Do I Do?

1 Pour enough bubble juice onto the cookie sheet to completely cover the bottom of it.

2 Dip the straw into the water, then put one end of it into the bubble juice on the cookie sheet.

3 Blow bubbles all over the cookie sheet, any way you want. Here are some of our favorite bubble games:

- Blow the biggest dome you can.
- Blow a dome inside a dome. Try to blow a dome inside a dome inside a dome.
- Blow a bubble caterpillar.
- Make the tallest pile of bubbles you can.
- Use the straw to blow bubbles in the air, and watch them bounce off a pile of bubbles on the cookie sheet.

Wow! I Didn't Know That!

Have you ever seen air bubbles in an ice cube? Bubbles trapped in the ice of glaciers contain air that can be hundreds of thousands of years old! When a part of a glacier splits off and falls into the ocean, the ice sizzles when these tiny bubbles pop. Scientists study these bubbles because the ancient air reveals a lot about what the earth's atmosphere was like a very long time ago.

Make sure anything that touches the bubble—your bubble blower, your hands—is wet. Bubbles pop when they touch something dry.

Handful of Bubbles

Experiment with bubbles while washing your hands!

What Do I Need?

- your hands
- water
- some liquid hand soap or dish washing soap
- straw

What Do I Do?

1 Get your hands wet. Squirt some liquid soap into your palm. Add some water, then rub your hands together. Make sure your hands are covered with soap and water.

2 Make a fist, then slide your fingers open to make an OK sign, like this:
Is there a soap film stretched across the O? If not, try again.

3 When you've got a soap film, blow gently through the O to blow a bubble. The bubble will stick to your hand. When you have a big enough bubble, gently squeeze your thumb and finger together to close the O. Then slowly turn your hand palm up.

4 You've got a bubble on your hand! What can you do with it? Here are a few ideas:

- Twist your hand so the bubble floats free. Another way to free the bubble is to blow on it slowly, until it moves up to the ends of your fingers and floats off into the air.

- Make sure your other hand is wet and soapy, then poke one finger through the bubble.

- Touch the bubble with the wet palm of your other hand. You can make a stretchy bubble accordion. How far can you stretch the bubble?

- Wet the end of a straw, then put it inside the bubble. Blow gently through the straw. Can you blow a bubble so big your whole hand is inside it? Can you blow a bubble bracelet all the way around your wrist?

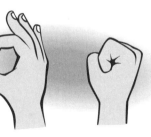

9

Bubble Prints

You can use bubbles to make art!

What Do I Need?

- newspaper
- bubble juice (see recipe on page 6)
- jars
- dish soap
- food coloring
- shallow bowl or pie tin
- straws
- paper

What Do I Do?

1 Put down a sheet of newspaper to keep your table clean.

2 Pour about half a cup of bubble juice into a jar. Add two extra squirts of dish soap. Choose the color you want your Bubble Print to be and add three or four really good squirts of that food coloring.

3 Swirl the liquid around in the jar until it's all mixed together, then pour about ½ inch into the shallow bowl.

4 Put one end of a straw in your mouth and put the other end of the straw into the deepest part of the liquid in the bowl. (Tilt the bowl a little if you need to make a deeper part.) Blow a big mound of bubbles. *Don't* suck in, or you'll get a mouthful of soap. Yuck!

5 Remove the straw and carefully lower a sheet of paper onto the mound of bubbles. Leave it for just a second, then lift it off. (Be careful that the paper touches only the bubbles, not the liquid.)

6 Let the paper dry, wet side up. (There may be bubbles on the paper, but don't worry. They'll pop as the paper dries.)

7 When the paper is dry, look at the shapes the bubbles made. Are there circles? Squares? Triangles? You can cut out the bubble shapes and hang them up, or use the paper as stationery.

For brighter colors, use liquid tempera paint instead of food coloring. Mix ¼ cup of paint with ½ cup of bubble juice.

8 If you want two-tone Bubble Prints, pour your prepared bubble juice into two bowls. Add one color of food coloring to one bowl and the other color to the second bowl. Make a Bubble Print with one color, then use the same piece of paper to make a second Bubble Print with the other color.

What's Going On?

What shapes can you find in your Bubble Prints?

Free-floating bubbles are usually round. This is because a sphere is the shape that provides the most space for the air inside the bubble with the least stretching of the elastic soap film.

When a bubble lands on a wet surface (like your hand or the water in a dishpan), it uses that surface as one wall and contracts to make a dome. When two bubble domes touch, the bubbles join, making a wall between them. This common wall lets each bubble's soap film contract a little, shrinking the bubble's surface area. A bubble in a cluster with other bubbles makes use of neighboring bubbles to minimize its own surface area.

When you make Bubble Prints, take a look at how the soap films in the print meet. They'll tend to come together in three-way junctions, with angles of about 120 degrees between the soap films. Since this is an arrangement that lets each soap film have the smallest possible surface area, the bubbles pull on each other and slip and slide until they settle into this configuration.

Like the soap films in a cluster of bubbles, the wax walls in a honeycomb meet in groups of three, forming 120-degree angles. That's the shape that provides the most space for honey while using the least wax.

Bubbularium

Make an observatory to see the amazing colors in bubbles.

What Do I Need?

- small clear plastic lid (from yogurt or margarine container)
- clear plastic tape
- flashlight that works
- bubble juice (see recipe on page 6)
- spoon
- straw
- room you can make dark

What Do I Do?

1 Tape the plastic lid over the end of the flashlight the light shines from.

2 Turn the flashlight on and hold it so the light shines straight up.

3 Dip your finger in the bubble juice and wet the lid. Put a spoonful of bubble juice on the lid. With a straw, blow one big bubble to make a bubble dome that covers the whole lid.

4 Turn off the lights and hold the flashlight so that the bottom of the bubble dome is just above your eyebrows.

5 Watch the swirling colors. If you put the wet straw into the bubble dome and blow very gently, you can move the colors around.

6 Watch the colors. How many do you see? If you watch a bubble for a few minutes, do the colors change? What colors do you see right before the bubble pops? Do you ever see black and white polka dots?

Wow! I Didn't Know That!

Right before it pops, the skin of a soap bubble is only one-millionth of an inch thick!

What's Going On?

Why are soap bubbles so colorful?

The colors of a soap bubble come from white light, which contains all the colors of the rainbow. When white light reflects from a soap film, some of the colors get brighter, and others disappear.

You can think of light as as being made up of waves—like the waves in the ocean. When scientists talk about waves, they often talk about a wave's frequency. Frequency is the number of times that a wave vibrates in a second. For ocean waves, frequency measures the number of times a passing wave makes a surfer bob up and down in a second. For light waves, frequency measures how many electromagnetic vibrations happen in a second.

The frequency of a light wave determines which color light you see. Violet light, for instance, is the highest frequency light that you can see; it vibrates 723,000 times in a billionth of a second. White light is made up of light waves of many different frequencies.

Two waves can be in the same place at the same time. Suppose two ocean waves of equal size meet. Each wave pushes up and down on the water in its path. Where the waves meet, there are two different forces acting on the water, one from each wave. If both waves push up on the water, the water moves twice as high as it would move if it were pushed by one wave alone. This is called *constructive interference*.

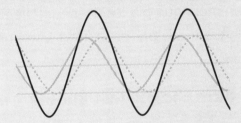

If one wave pushes up and the other pushes down, the two pushes cancel each other and the water doesn't move at all. When this happens, it's called *destructive interference*.

What does all this have to do with the colors of bubbles? Light waves, like water waves, can interfere with each other. A bubble film is a sort of sandwich: a layer of soap molecules, a filling of water molecules, and then another layer of soap molecules. When light waves reflecting from one layer of soap molecules meet up with light waves reflecting from the second layer of soap molecules, the two sets of waves interfere. Some waves add together, making certain frequencies or colors of light brighter. Other waves cancel each other, removing a frequency or color from the mixture. The colors that you see are what's left after the light waves interfere. They're called *interference colors*.

The interference colors depend on how far the light waves have to travel before they meet up again—and that depends on the distance between the layers or the thickness of the soap film. Each color corresponds to a certain thickness of the soap film. By causing the liquid bubble film to flow and change in thickness, a puff of wind makes the bubble colors swirl and change.

The very thinnest film—one that's only a few millionths of an inch thick—looks black because all the reflecting wavelengths of light cancel. When the soap film looks black, it's just about to pop.

What's the best set-up for seeing colors in a bubble?

Interference colors on a bubble look brightest when there's white light shining on the bubble and a black background behind it. The colors come from light that's reflecting from the soap film. You want to be on the same side of the bubble as the light source so that light will bounce back to your eyes. The black background keeps light that's shining through from the other side of the bubble from washing out the colors.

Where else can I see shimmering colors like these?

You can experiment with interference colors using Reflecting Rainbows (page 18) and making Rainbow Prints (page 20).

What Else Can I Do with Bubbles?

You're on your way to becoming a bubble expert. If you want to keep on exploring and experimenting with bubbles, here are other things you can try.

Find the Best Bubble Blower

What makes a good bubble blower? Something that has holes that air can blow through. Try using a big, slotted serving spoon. Dip it in your bubble juice and wave it through the air to make many tiny bubbles. Or use the plastic basket that strawberries come in.

Tubes of just about any size are also great for bubble blowing. Ask a grown-up to use a can opener to cut both ends off a can. Dip one end of the can in the bubble juice to make a soap film over the opening. Then blow in the other end.

Bubbles for Lunch?

Bubbles make the holes in Swiss cheese. Bubbles make bread rise so that it's light and fluffy. See if you can make a lunch that has only bubbly foods. What other foods have bubbles in them? Maybe a Swiss cheese sandwich, a glass of bubbly ginger ale, and lemon meringue pie for dessert. (The fluffy meringue that's on top is filled with bubbles.)

Blow the Biggest Bubble

See how big a bubble you can blow. Here's a hint: when you blow hard, you're more likely to make lots of little bubbles (or no bubbles at all). To make a big bubble, try blowing gently.

14

It's Colorific!

Without color, the world would be a much duller place. This picture is in black and white—but *you* can find a real rainbow—with rainbow colors.

Paul Doherty, a physicist and teacher who works at the Exploratorium, looks for rainbows wherever he goes. He looks for them in the sky after it rains—but he also finds them in lawn sprinklers, waterfalls, and fountains.

Paul knows where to look for rainbows. You can't just stand anywhere and stare at the water in the sprinkler and find a rainbow. You have to stand in the right place and know where to look. But if you know how, you can find a rainbow anytime you've got water drops and sunshine. (See page 16 to learn the secret.)

Paul's always looking for the secret colors that other people overlook. In puddles in the street, he sometimes finds a little bit of oil or gasoline floating on the water's surface. The oil reflects beautiful shimmering colors—like the colors of a soap bubble. Late in the day, he watches for the *green flash,* the green light that sometimes appears just as the sun dips below the horizon.

Paul says that even after years and years of looking for interesting colors, he still finds new places to see them. On the beach, he knows he'll see shimmering colors inside an abalone shell—but he's surprised to find some of the same colors reflecting from a broad leaf of seaweed. Once you start looking, Paul says, you can find amazing colors in the most unexpected places.

At the Exploratorium, we don't just look for unexpected colors. Sometimes, we make colors appear—right where we want them. In this chapter, you'll discover how to find colors and make them in places you never expected.

Physicist Paul Doherty is looking for rainbows in a fountain. The dome in the background is the rotunda of the Exploratorium. To find out why Paul is holding his hands like that, see page 16.

Rainbows on Your Lawn

If you know where to look, you can find a rainbow in your garden sprinkler or in the spray of a fountain.

What Do I Need?

- a hose that can spray, a sprinkler, or a fountain
- a warm, sunny day

What Do I Do?

1 Stand near the spray of water drops. Stand with your back to the sun. Find your shadow. It should be between you and the spray. If it isn't, move around until it is.

2 Look for a rainbow in the spray.

Wow! I Didn't Know That!

When you look at a rainbow, you see seven colors. They are always in the same order—**r**ed, **o**range, **y**ellow, **g**reen, **b**lue, **i**ndigo, and **v**iolet. An easy way to remember the colors and the order is to think of the name ROY G. BIV, spelled from the first letter of each color.

3 If you don't see a rainbow, here's how to find one. Look for the shadow of your head. Hold both arms straight out in front of you. Spread your hands as wide as they will stretch with your thumbs touching, tip to tip. Place the tip of one little finger so that its shadow falls in the center of the shadow of your head.

Keeping that little finger in place, look at the sunlit drops that line up with your other little finger. You should see a rainbow right there.

4 When you move, the rainbow moves with you. Someone standing next to you may also see a rainbow in the spray, but their rainbow will be in a slightly different place. Each person sees his or her own personal rainbow.

If you do this with your family, ask everyone to point to the top of the rainbow they see. Each of you will be pointing to a different spot.

What's Going On?

Why does sunlight shining through water drops make a rainbow?

Whenever light moves from air into something clear (like water or glass), it slows down just a little bit. If it hits the water or glass at an angle, it bends as it slows down. This bending is called *refraction*.

Just how much light bends when it hits water or glass depends partly on the color of the light. The white light of the sun is made up of all the colors of the rainbow. When this sunlight reflects off water drops (or shines through a prism), each of these colors bends at a slightly different angle, fanning out to make a rainbow.

Why do I have to stand with my back to the sun to see a rainbow?

To make a rainbow, sunlight has to shine into a raindrop (bending as it moves from the air into the water), bounce off the far side of the drop, and then leave the drop (bending again as it moves from the water to the air). So if you're going to see a rainbow, you have to be standing where your eyes can intercept this colored light. That means you have to stand with your back to the sun, so that the sunlight is shining into the raindrops from over your shoulder.

Knowing this helps you know when to look for rainbows in the sky. You're likely to see a rainbow when the sun is low in the western sky and sunlight is shining on raindrops to the east. At the same time of day, you won't see a rainbow in raindrops that are west of you. That's because you're facing into the sun.

What else can I see when I'm looking for rainbows?

If conditions are right, you may see two rainbows—one inside the other. The inner, brighter arc is the primary rainbow; the dimmer, outer arc is the secondary rainbow. Notice the order of the colors in your rainbow. In the primary rainbow, red is on the outside of the arc and violet is on the inside. In the secondary rainbow, the colors are in the same sequence, but violet is on the outside and red is on the inside.

Reflecting Rainbows

Decorate your white walls with rainbow colors!

What Do I Need?

- compact disc (also known as a CD) (If you don't own any CDs, you can buy an old one at a garage sale. Or ask at a record store if they will give you a CD that won't play.)
- sunshine (or a bright flashlight and a room that you can make dark)
- piece of white paper

What Do I Do?

1 Take the CD out of its case and take a look at the blank side (the side that doesn't have any printing on it). You'll see bands of shimmering color. Tilt the CD back and forth and the colors will shift and change.

2 Hold the CD in the sunshine. Or if it's a cloudy day, turn out the lights and shine your flashlight at the CD. Hold your piece of white paper so that the light reflecting off the CD shines onto the paper. The reflected light will make fabulous rainbow colors on your paper.

> Be careful! Don't reflect the sunlight into your eyes or anyone else's eyes. The reflected sunlight is so bright that it can injure your eyes.

3 Tip the CD and see how that changes the reflections. Change the distance from the CD to the paper. What happens to the colors?

4 Take a close look at your CD. It's made of aluminum coated with plastic. The colors that you see on the CD are created by white light reflecting from ridges in the metal.

The Home Scientists in the Manley family had their whole neighborhood lined up to try this. "We would have had fights if we hadn't had three CDs," they said. They liked all the different designs and shapes the reflected light made. The Sandoval family tried this under the covers with a flashlight on a cloudy morning. Mom liked this experiment, because she could slip away while the kids kept playing.

What's Going On?

Why does a CD reflect rainbow colors?

Like water drops in falling rain, the CD separates white light into all the colors that make it up. The colors you see reflecting from a CD are interference colors, like the shifting colors you see on a soap bubble or an oil slick.

You can think of light as as being made up of waves—like the waves in the ocean. When light waves reflect off the ridges on your CD, they overlap and interfere with each other. Sometimes the waves add together, making certain colors brighter, and sometimes they cancel each other, taking certain colors away. To find out more about light waves and how they interfere with each other, see page 13.

More Things to Do

When light reflects off or passes through something with many small ridges or scratches, you often get rainbow colors and interesting patterns. These are called *interference patterns.* Here are several other ways you can see interference patterns.

- Squint at a distant bright light at night. You'll see starburst patterns around the light. If you look closely, you can see colors in the patterns. These patterns form when light bends around your eyelashes and imperfections in the layers that make up the lens of your eye. Tilt your head to one side while watching the pattern and notice that the pattern moves with you.

- In a dark room, look at a bright light (maybe a candle flame) through a nylon stocking, a silk scarf, a feather, or a tea strainer. The pattern that you see depends on what you look through. Move the thing you're looking through and notice that the pattern moves with it.

- Buy a set of "rainbow glasses" in a toy store or a science shop. Through these glasses, all lights look like rainbows. The glasses are made with *diffraction gratings*, clear plastic that is etched with many lines.

Rainbow Prints

Add a clear coating to black paper, and get a rainbow of amazing colors!

What Do I Need?

- pie tin or shallow bowl
- water
- scissors
- construction paper (dark colors—like black, brown, or blue—work best)
- bottle of *clear* nail polish
- paper towels or newspaper

What Do I Do?

1 Fill the shallow bowl with about an inch of water.

2 Cut out pieces of construction paper. Make sure they're small enough to fit in the bowl.

3 Put one piece of paper into the water. Press it down with your fingers until it's completely wet. When you let go, it may float to the top of the water. That's okay. When black paper gets wet, some of its color may come off in the water. That's okay, too.

4 Pull the brush out of the bottle of clear nail polish. Touch the very tip of the brush to the water. You should see a film floating on the water. (If you don't, add *one* more drop of nail polish.)

5 Make sure the film is floating on top of the paper. Then very carefully and slowly lift the piece of paper out of the water. Tilt it a little so the water runs off. Gently lay it onto a paper towel or some newspaper to dry.

6 If you have different colors of paper, make more Rainbow Prints. Start with fresh water each time.

7 When your prints are dry, pick one up and hold it under a bright light or out in the sun. Do you see the colors? Tilt the paper until you see the brightest colors. Wow! The colors of the print will be a little different with each color paper you use.

Color Watch

Where else can you see colors like these? If you're in a city, look for oil slicks in dark puddles on a rainy day. Hummingbirds, pigeons, and many other birds have feathers on their throats that make these shimmery colors. You can also see these colors in soap bubbles, on the shells of some insects, and on the scales of some kinds of fish.

Wow! I Didn't Know That!

The scientific name for the pattern of colors on your Rainbow Prints is *iridescence.* That word comes from the Greek word *iris,* which means "rainbow." In Greek myths, Iris was a goddess who traveled down the rainbow to bring messages to the people on earth.

The Home Scientists in the Blair-Stolk family used their Rainbow Prints to make a paper butterfly with wings made of many iridescent "scales" of torn paper.

What's Going On?

Why does clear nail polish on dark-colored paper reflect colors?

In this experiment, the layer of nail polish on the paper is much thinner than the layer you get when you brush on nail polish. This very thin layer of nail polish can reveal the hidden colors of white light.

When you look at a Rainbow Print, you see the light that reflects from the clear nail polish. Some of this light is reflecting from the top surface, where the nail polish meets the air. Some is reflecting from the bottom surface, where the nail polish meets the paper. The light waves reflecting from these two surfaces overlap.

Like the light waves reflecting from the CD or from a soap bubble, light waves reflecting from the nail polish can add together to make a brighter color. Or they can subtract from each other, taking a color away from the mixture. The colors that you see are the ones that are left over when some colors are subtracted from white light.

The colors you see depend partly on the thickness of the layer of nail polish. Nail polish films of different thicknesses reflect different colors to your eyes.

You can change the colors you see by tilting the paper. This changes the angle of the light that's reflecting off the nail polish and into your eyes. At different angles, different light waves add or subtract—and you'll see different colors.

Black Magic

Discover the secret colors hidden in a black marker!

What Do I Need?

- scissors
- white paper coffee filter
- black marker (*not* permanent)
- water
- coffee cup or mug

What Do I Do?

1 Cut a circle out of the coffee filter. (It doesn't have to be a perfect circle, just a round shape that's about as big as your spread-out hand.

2 With the black marker, draw a line across the circle, about 1 inch up from the bottom.

3 Put some water in the cup— enough to cover the bottom. Curl the paper circle so it fits inside the cup. Make sure the bottom of the circle is in the water.

4 Watch as the water flows up the paper. When it touches the black line, you'll start to see some different colors.

5 Leave the paper in the water until the colors go all the way to the top edge. How many colors can you see?

6 If you have another black marker, draw a line on a clean, dry coffee filter circle. Put the circle in some fresh water. Does this marker make different colors than the first one?

Center Stage

Use a clean, dry coffee filter circle. Use your marker to draw a black spot in the center. Put the circle on a saucer, and put a few drops of water on the spot. In a few minutes you'll see rings of color that go out from the center of the circle to the edges. Our picture is in black and white, but when you do this, you'll see some amazing colors.

What's Going On?

How does Black Magic work? Why do some black inks separate into many colors on a wet coffee filter?

Most nonpermanent markers use inks that are made of colored pigments and water. On a coffee filter, the water in the ink carries the pigment onto the paper. When the ink dries, the pigment remains on the paper.

When you dip the paper in water, the dried pigments dissolve. As the water travels up the paper, it carries the pigments along with it. Different-colored pigments are carried along at different rates; some travel farther and faster than others. How fast each pigment travels depends on the size of the pigment molecule and on how strongly the pigment is attracted to the paper. Since the water carries the different pigments at different rates, the black ink separates to reveal the colors that were mixed to make it.

In this experiment, you're using a technique called *chromatography*. The name comes from the Greek words *chroma* and *graph* for "color writing." The technique was developed in 1910 by Russian botanist Mikhail Tsvet. He used it for separating the pigments that made up plant dyes.

There are many different types of chromatography. In all of them, a gas or liquid (like the water in your ex-periment) flows through a stationary substance (like your coffee filter). Since different ingredients in a mixture are carried along at different rates, they end up in different places. By examining where all the ingredients ended up, scientists can figure out what was combined to make the mixture.

Chromatography is one of the most valuable techniques biochemists have for separating mixtures. It can be used to determine the ingredients that make up a particular flavor or scent, to analyze the components of pollutants, to find traces of drugs in urine, and to separate blood proteins in various species of animals (a technique that's used to determine evolutionary relationships).

Why does mixing many colors of ink make black?

Ink and paint get their colors by absorbing some of the colors in white light and reflecting others. Green ink looks green because it reflects the green part of white light and absorbs all the other colors. Red ink looks red because it reflects red light and absorbs all the other colors. When you mix green, red, blue, and yellow ink, each ink that you add absorbs more light. That leaves less light to reflect to your eye. Since the mixture absorbs light of many colors and reflects very little, you end up with black.

What Else Can I Do with Color?

In this chapter, you've found colors that are hidden in white light and colors that are hidden in black ink. If you want to keep exploring, here are some other things to try.

Crazy Mixed-Up Colors

Get some watercolor paints and mix different colors together. Mix a blob of red paint with a blob of yellow paint. What color do you get? What happens when you mix blue and yellow? Try to make black by mixing paints together.

Here's a question about mixing colors that will stump most people—including most grown-ups. What color do you get when you mix all the colors together?

That's a tricky question. The answer depends on exactly what you're mixing—colored lights or colored paints.

When you mix paints of all the colors of the rainbow together, you get a very dark muddy color. If you mix just the right amount of each color, you get a color that's pretty close to black.

That's what happens when you mix paint. But when you mix light, the answer is different. Sunlight is made of all the colors of the rainbow—that's why you get a rainbow when sunlight shines through water drops. So if you took lights of all different colors and mixed just the right amount of each color together, you'd get white light like the light from the sun.

The Sunday Comics—Up Close

With a magnifying glass, you can take a close look at some colors—and find out something surprising.

First, look at the Sunday comics through a magnifying glass. All the colors that you see are made from tiny dots of ink. Without the magnifying glass, Charlie Brown's face is pink. Through the magnifying glass, you'll see dots of reddish ink with white between them. Without the magnifying glass, all those tiny colored dots blend together so your eye sees pink.

Now use your magnifying glass to look at the screen of a color TV for a few seconds. You'll see tiny strips or dots of red, blue, and green. All the other colors that you see when you're watching a color TV are made from these three colors mixed together.

3 SEEING THE LIGHT

Take a look out your window on a sunny day. What do you see?

No matter where you are, one answer is always true. Bob Miller, an artist who built many of the Exploratorium's exhibits on light, figured it out years ago. Bob says that no matter where you are, you see light. In fact, light is the only thing you *can* see.

Take a look at your eyes in a mirror. In the middle of each eye there's a colored circle called the *iris.* In the middle of each iris there's a black spot called the *pupil.* The pupil is a hole that lets light into your eye.

Light from the sun shines on trees, flowers, cars, and the pages of this book. Some of this light bounces into your eyes, shining in through your pupils. Your eyes use that light to make a picture of the world. You see trees, flowers, cars, or this book when light bounces off these things and gets into your eyes.

The same thing happens in a camera—light shines in through a hole and makes a picture of the world. In a camera, that picture is captured on film. In your eyes, the picture shines on your *retinas,* the light-sensitive screens at the backs of your eyes. Information from your retinas travels to your brain, and then you see the world.

In this chapter, you can experiment with using light to make pictures of the world—and learn a little bit about how light lets you see.

I'm going to take apart this camera to find out how it uses light to make pictures of the world!

Bob Miller is an artist who has spent a lot of time thinking about light. He says that light is the only thing you can see. Light shines in through your pupils, the dark spot in the center of each eye, and paints a picture of the world.

25

Taking Apart a Camera

Working with a grown-up, you can take apart a disposable camera and figure out how it works.

What Do I Need?

- flat-bladed screwdriver or a butter knife
- used disposable camera *without* a flash. You can get one for free from most one-hour film developing stores or camera stores. Try to get two or three of the same kind of camera so that you can compare the one that you take apart to one that's still in one piece.

DANGER!

Do not try to take apart a disposable camera that includes a flash. You can get a shock strong enough to kill you by poking a screwdriver into the wrong area of a flash camera. Taking apart a camera without a flash is safe, as long as you make sure no one swallows any of the little pieces.

What Do I Do?

1 Find the camera's viewfinder, the shutter-release button (the button you push to take a picture), the wheel you turn to advance the film, and (looking at the front of the camera) the lens.

2 Take a good look at how the plastic pieces that make the body of the camera fit together. Look for seams into which you could slide the flat tip of your screwdriver or the blade of your knife. Look for snaps or latches that hold the plastic pieces together. These cameras aren't made to be taken apart, but they pop apart fairly easily if you pry in the right spot.

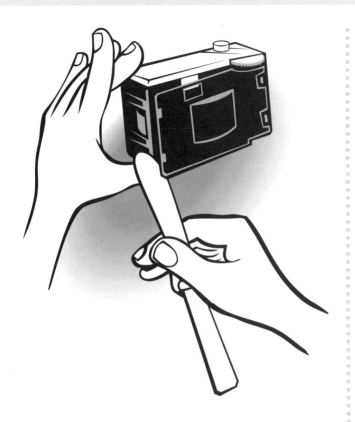

The film starts out in the film compartment on the left. It stretches across the rectangular opening in the middle, then winds around a spool in the film compartment on the right. Turning the film advance wheel pulls film onto the spool in the film compartment on the right. Pushing the shutter-release button briefly opens the *aperture,* the opening that lets light shine through the lens.

4 Push the shutter release button right now. Do you hear a click? Probably not. To make the shutter work, you need to cock a spring that's inside the camera. Look right above the rectangular opening in the middle of the camera for a sprocket wheel. The sprockets on this wheel fit into holes in the edge of the film. When the camera has film in it, this sprocket wheel is turned as you advance the film.

3 Carefully pry the back off the camera. Without the back, the camera will look something like this:

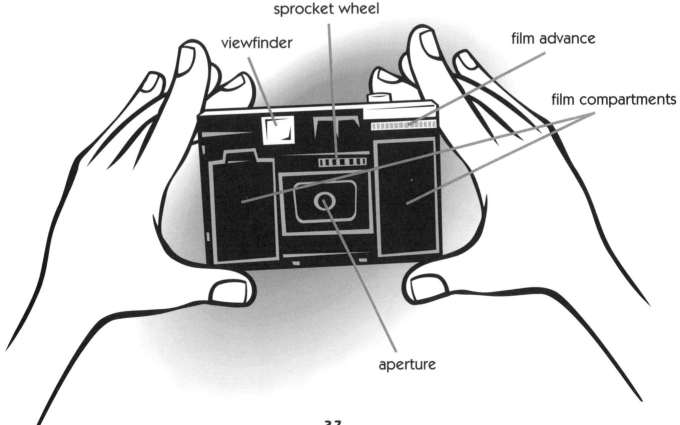

sprocket wheel

viewfinder

film advance

film compartments

aperture

5 To cock the spring and make the shutter work, you need to turn the sprocket wheel. Keep turning until you hear a click. Push the shutter-release button again. You should hear the shutter open and close with a click. If it doesn't, turn the sprocket wheel until you hear a couple of clicks and try again.

6 Turn the sprocket wheel again. Hold the camera up to the light and look through the aperture as you push the shutter release button. You'll see a flash of light as the shutter opens and closes.

To find out how this flash of light lets the camera take pictures, see page 29.

7 Pry the front off the camera. Be careful not to lose the lens! It may fall off when you pry off the front.

Turn the sprocket wheel again. Push the shutter release button while looking at the camera from the front. You'll see the shutter open and close. You can pull the shutter open and see the opening that lets light into the camera.

8 If you haven't already found the camera's lens, look for it now. It's probably on the front of the camera. Take it off the camera and you can use it for your next experiment.

Wow! I Didn't Know That!

In Greek, *photo* means "light" and *graph* means "picture." Put those two words together and you have the word *photograph*—a picture made from light.

What's Going On?

How does a camera take a picture?

When you push the shutter release button on your camera, the shutter snaps open for a fraction of a second, letting a flash of light into the camera. That light shines through the camera's lens and makes a picture of the world on the film. The chemicals in the film react to the light, capturing the picture.

You can use the lens from the camera and make pictures from light (though you can't easily capture them on film). Just follow the instructions on page 30.

How does a lens make a picture from light?

Suppose you follow the instructions on page 30 and use your lens to make a picture of your TV screen. The picture on your TV is made of many tiny points of light. (You can see this if you hold the lens near your TV screen and look through the lens at the TV picture.) The light shining from each of these points on the TV screen spreads out in all directions. To make an image of the TV picture, you need to gather some of this light so that it's all in the same place again.

Your lens does exactly that. It takes light that's shining out in all directions from one spot, and bends it so that it all comes back together. When light from one point on your TV screen shines through your lens, the lens bends the light so that it comes back together at a point on the other side of the lens. On the other side of the lens, all these points of light make a picture that looks just like the picture on the TV screen, but upside down.

Suppose you use your lens to make a picture of something else—a bouquet of flowers, for example. Light reflects off the white petal of a flower and shines in all directions. Some of that light shines through your

lens. Your lens bends all this light so that it comes back together on the other side of the lens at a single place—making a white spot at that place.

Sunshine also bounces off the blue vase that's holding the flowers. Your lens bends all this light so that it comes back together on the other side of the lens—making a blue spot. These spots—along with the green spots from the flower's leaves and other blue spots from the vase and white spots from the petals—line up on the other side of the lens to make an image of the bouquet.

When you focus the image on your screen, you are searching for the place where your lens bends all the light from one spot on the bouquet so that it comes back together to make one sharply focused spot on your paper screen. Where exactly is that place? That depends on the distance between your lens and the bouquet and the distance between your lens and the screen. You can focus an image on the screen either by moving the screen relative to the bouquet or by moving the lens relative to the screen. Either way, you are arranging things so that the screen is in just the right place for your particular lens.

What does a camera have to do with how I see the world?

In many ways, your eye is similar to a camera. When you look at the world, light shines through the cornea, the clear tough covering that protects your eye, and then through the pupil, the dark hole that's right in the center of the iris, the colored part of your eye. This light then shines through your eye's lens, and the lens focuses an image of the world on your retina, a layer of light-sensitive cells at the back of your eye. These light-sensitive cells detect the image focused by the lens and send a message to your brain. Your brain analyzes the information from the retina—and you see the world.

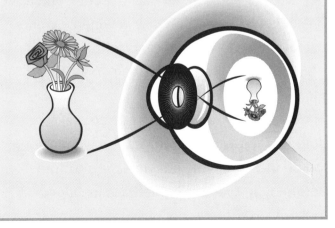

Pictures from Light

With a lens, you can bend light to make pictures of the world.

What Do I Need?

- lens—like the one in a magnifying glass or one from a disposable camera
- room that you can make very dark
- light source—like a TV set or a brightly lit window
- sheet of white paper

> If you take your lens outside and focus a bright spot of light, DON'T stare at the bright spot or hold it in one place for more than a few seconds. This can hurt your eyes or start a fire!

What Do I Do?

1 Look through your lens at these words or at your fingertip. Do things look bigger through your lens? If they do, your lens is a magnifying lens. It will work for this experiment.

2 Go into a room that has just one source of light. On a sunny day, a window works just fine. (Turn off any electric lights in the room.) At night, you can turn on your TV set and use it as a light source.

You're going to use your lens to make a picture of the light source. So you want a light source that will make an interesting picture. A picture of an ordinary lightbulb is just a round spot, which is pretty boring.

3 Stand a few feet away from your light source. Hold your lens up so that light can shine through it. Hold the piece of paper on the other side of the lens so that light shines through the lens and onto the paper.

The paper is your screen—like the screen in a movie theater. The paper screen will reflect a picture made of light so that you can see it.

4 Start with the lens up close to the paper, and slowly move it away from the paper and toward the light source. Watch the pattern of light on the paper. When the lens is the right distance from the paper, you'll see a picture of the light source. The picture will be upside down and backward.

5 If you don't see a picture right away, keep trying. Try standing closer to the light source. Or try moving the lens farther from the paper. It may take some experimenting, but sooner or later you'll get a picture.

What's Going On?

Warning

You may already know that you can use a lens to focus sunlight into a very bright circle. That circle can be hot enough to start a fire. For many kids, playing with a lens outdoors can be like playing with matches. Take appropriate precautions.

If you take a lens outside and use it to focus a circle of sunlight, DON'T stare at the bright spot. That spot of light is an image of the sun. You can hurt your eyes by staring at it, just as you can hurt your eyes by staring at the sun.

To find out how a lens makes a picture from light, see page 29.

Wow! I Didn't Know That!

When you use your lens to make a picture of something that's brightly lit, you are doing the same thing that a movie projector does. In a movie projector, a light shines through a transparent picture, then through a lens. The lens takes the light from the picture and makes a big picture on the movie screen.

Pringles® Pinhole
Recycle a potato chip can into a simple camera!

What Do I Need?

- empty Pringles® chip can
- marker
- ruler
- X-Acto knife or utility knife (ask a grown-up to help you cut)
- thumbtack or pushpin
- masking tape
- aluminum foil
- scissors (if you want)
- bright sunny day

What Do I Do?

1 Take the plastic lid off the Pringles® can and wipe out the inside. (Save the lid!)

2 Draw a line with the marker all the way around the can, about 2 inches up from the bottom. Have a grown-up cut along that line so the tube is in two pieces.

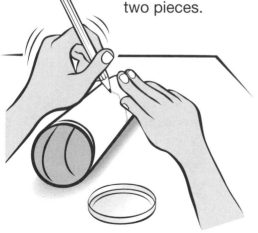

3 The shorter bottom piece has a metal end. With the thumbtack, make a hole in the center of the metal.

4 Put the plastic lid onto the shorter piece. Put the longer piece back on top. Tape all the pieces together.

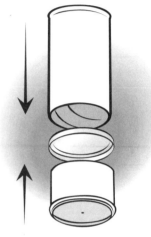

5 To keep light out of the tube, use a piece of aluminum foil that's about 1 foot long. Tape one end of the foil to the tube. Wrap the foil all the way around the tube twice, then tape the loose edge of the foil closed. If you have extra foil at the top, just tuck it neatly inside the tube.

6 Go outside on a sunny day. Close one eye and hold the tube up to your other eye. You want the inside of the tube to be as dark as possible—so cup your hands around the opening of the tube if you need to.

Look around your yard through the tube. The lid makes a screen that shows you upside-down color pictures!

7 Hold your hand below the tube and move it very slowly upward. Your hand is moving *up,* but you'll see its shadow move *down* the screen!

My whole family is upside down!

Wow! I Didn't Know That!

You've made a camera! This kind of camera is called a *camera obscura*—which is Latin for "dark chamber." The first camera obscuras were small rooms that were completely dark except for a tiny hole in a wall that let in a dot of sunlight. People in the room saw an image of the trees and sky on the wall opposite the hole—and were amazed when the image disappeared at sunset!

The Home Scientists in the Graff family improved their Pringles® Pinhole by using a foam soda can holder as an eyepiece. It made the inside of the tube dark, and was easier to use for people who wear glasses.

What's Going On?

How does a hole in the bottom of a Pringles® can make a picture of the world?

The hole doesn't make the picture. The image of the world is always there. All the hole does is make it possible for you to see it.

Suppose you point your Pringles® Pinhole at a brightly lit bouquet of flowers. Light reflects off the red rose, the blue iris, the white daisy, and the green leaves. If you hold a piece of white paper near the bouquet, some of that reflected light will shine on the paper—but it won't look like anything. That's because light bouncing off the red rose ends up overlapping with light bouncing off the blue iris, the white daisy, and the green leaves. There are many images of the bouquet on the paper—but they overlap with one another, and the colors all blend together, making a jumble of light.

The hole isolates a small part of the light, sorting a single image from the jumble. Only a few of the light rays reflecting off each point on the rose are traveling in a direction that will let them pass through the hole. The same is true for light bouncing off all the other flowers in the bouquet. On the other side of the hole, these light rays reveal an image of the bouquet.

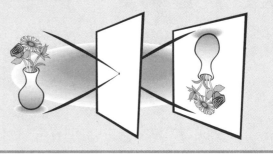

Seeing in the Dark

When it's dark, your eyes adjust to the light.

WHAT BIG EYES YOU HAVE

What Do I Need?

- mirror
- room that you can make dark

What Do I Do?

1 Stand in front of the mirror. Turn off the lights so that the room is dark and count to 20.

2 Turn the lights back on and watch your pupils—the black spots in the middle of your eyes. Do you see them change?

Each pupil is a hole that lets light into your eye. When it's dark, the pupil gets bigger, to let more light in. When the light is brighter, the pupil shrinks.

DISAPPEARING COLORS

What Do I Need?

- room you can make dark
- radio (if you want)
- small pieces of paper in four or five different colors
- black marker
- colored markers or crayons
- white paper

What Do I Do?

1 Read all these instructions. (Once you turn off the lights, you won't be able to read them!)

2 Turn off all the lights in the room. It should be as dark as possible.

3 Sit in the room for 10 to 15 minutes, until your eyes adjust to the dark. You should be able to see the shapes of pieces of furniture but not much detail.

(Sitting in the dark for that long can be boring, so you may want to listen to the radio or ask someone to tell you a story.)

4 Look at the pieces of construction paper. Can you tell what color each piece is? Use the black marker to write your guess on each piece.

5 Look at the colored markers. Can you tell what color each one of them is? Use each marker to write the color you think it is. If you think you're holding the red marker, write "red" on the white paper.

6 Now turn on the lights. How did you do? If you're like most people, you probably mixed up most of the colors.

Wow! I Didn't Know That!

In dim light, your eyes can't see colors—just blacks, whites, and grays. That's the way an *achromat*—a person who can't see colors—sees the world all the time. Knut Nordby is a vision researcher and an achromat. When he was a kid, he happily colored the sky green, yellow, or pink, and colored grass orange or dark blue. His pictures looked strange to the other kids, but they matched the way the world looked to Knut.

What's Going On?

Why can I see better after ten minutes in the dark? And why can't I see colors in dim light?

Since your eyes use light to make pictures of the world, you need light to see. You can't see if it's really dark, as dark as the inside of a closet with the door closed. But in most situations that we call dark, there's still some light—from the moon, the stars, or a streetlight shining in the window. For your eyes to make use of that limited light, you need to give them time.

When you step into a dark place, your pupils expand, letting more light into your eyes. That happens right away. But other changes that help you see in dim light take longer.

You see the world because light-sensitive cells in your eye detect patterns of light and darkness and relay this information to your brain. Your eyes have two different types of light-sensitive cells: *rods* and *cones*. In bright light, your vision depends on the cones; in dimmer light, you use the rods.

After five or ten minutes in the dark, your eyes are relying almost entirely on the rods. The rods register the pattern of light on the retina—they can distinguish bright light from dim light—but they don't distinguish one color from another. That's why you can't distinguish colors in dim light.

A trick to try

After your eyes are used to the dark, you'll have better luck seeing details if you don't stare directly at what you want to see. When you stare directly at something, its image falls on an area of your eye that's packed with cones but has very few rods. To see a dim star in the night sky, astronomers look slightly above or below it. The star's image falls on an area of the eye that has more rods than cones, providing a better view.

What Else Can I Do with Light and Lenses?

You don't need any special equipment to keep experimenting. You can find what you need to make lenses right in your own kitchen.

Make a lens from a water drop

Put a drop of water on a piece of plastic wrap or a clear lid. Put the lid on top of a piece of newspaper. Can you read the words through the drop of water? Now lift up the lid, very slowly. What happens to the words?

Use your water drop lens to look at other things around your house. The drop of water makes things look bigger—it magnifies them—just like the lens from the disposable camera did. That's because a drop of water and the camera lens are both convex lenses. Most convex lenses are clear and curved, and are thicker in the middle than they are at the edges.

Make a lens from a jar

Get a glass jar with smooth sides. Make sure it has a lid. The jar is clear, and it's curved. Is it a lens? You can test it by seeing if it makes things look different. Try putting it on its side on top of a piece of newspaper. Look through the glass. Do the words look bigger?

Now fill the jar with water, all the way to the top, then put the lid on tight. Turn the jar on its side and put it on top of the newspaper again. Look at the words through the water-filled jar. Are the words bigger, or just wider? If you turn the jar around, do the words look taller?

A water-filled jar with straight sides is a cylindrical lens. It makes things look bigger in one direction, but not in another.

Can you think of other things in your house that would make interesting lenses?

SEEING ISN'T BELIEVING

I can see the face of the man in the moon. With the experiments in this chapter, you can see a lot of other cool things, too.

A lot of people say "seeing is believing." They think that when they look at the world, they see what's really there.

At the Exploratorium, we don't believe everything we see. We've learned that sometimes you don't see what's really there—and sometimes you see things that aren't there at all.

Take a look at the picture of a house. It's an ordinary house, but do you see something else, too? Most people think that this house looks like a face—with two windows for eyes, a basketball hoop for a nose, and a garage door for a mouth. You know that it's not a face. You know it's a house. But once you think that the windows look like eyes, it's hard *not* to see the face.

You're used to seeing faces. You've probably carved faces on jack-o'-lanterns or drawn them with crayons. So it's easy to see faces that aren't really there—like the face on the house or the face of the man in the moon.

Is it a house or is it a face?

That's because your eyes and brain work together to let you see the world. Your eyes make a picture of the world, and your brain tries to make sense of that picture. Your brain works really hard to make sense of what you see. One of the ways that your brain makes its job easier is to put the things you see into familiar patterns. The house looks kind of like a face—so your brain tells you that you see a face.

To learn how your eyes and brain work, it's fun to take a look at pictures that fool your eyes and brain so that you see something unexpected. Along the way, you'll find out why movies look like they move (even though they're really just a bunch of still pictures), how your two eyes work together to make one picture of the world, and why sometimes you see mysterious shapes floating in the blue sky.

Floaters

If you look up at the sky, you can see what's inside your eyes!

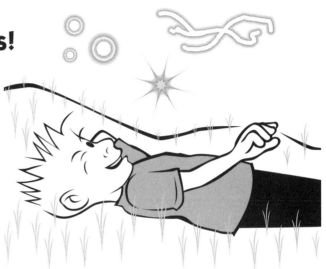

What Do I Need?

- your eyes
- dry, clear day

What Do I Do?

1 Go outside and lie down on the ground.

2 Relax. Just look up at the sky or at the clouds. (*Don't* look at the sun!)

3 After a while, you'll probably see tiny shapes floating in the air. They may look like specks of light, clear circles, or even a tangle of clear threads.

4 Close one eye. Are the floating shapes still there? Open that eye and close the other. Some of the floating shapes may disappear when you close each eye.

What's Going On?

What are those things that I see drifting in the blue sky?

These drifting forms, known as *floaters*, are caused by bits of junk drifting in the liquid near your eye's *retina*, the layer of light-sensitive cells at the back of your eye. Some of this junk may be remnants of structures that were part of your eye when you were just an embryo. Some of it may be remnants of red blood cells that leaked out of the blood vessels that supply the retina. Once these blood cells are floating, they lose their color and swell into spheres. Sometimes they form strings; sometimes they float alone.

These floaters move when the liquid in your eye moves. When you lie on your back, the floaters sink and drift closer to your retina and may settle into the depression of the *fovea*, the area of the retina where your vision is the sharpest.

While you're staring at the blue sky, you may also notice tiny bright specks moving against the blue. They seem to follow regular pathways, moving jerkily in single file in time to the beating of your heart. These wandering specks are blood cells, moving through the blood vessels that nourish the retina.

Hot Dog Finger

See a mysterious hot dog that seems to float in midair!

What Do I Need?

- your fingers
- your eyes

What Do I Do?

1 Hold your arms out in front of you. Stick out the first finger on each hand. Point the tips of your fingers at each other and hold the fingers about 10 inches in front of your nose.

2 Bring your fingers closer together—slowly. Keep both eyes open, but don't look right at your fingers. Look at a spot a few feet beyond them.

What's Going On?

How does Hot Dog Finger work? Why do you need two eyes to see this illusion?

Your two eyes give you slightly different views of the world. To prove it to yourself, close your right eye and point to something across the room. Without moving your pointing finger, open your right eye and close your left eye. Your finger will no longer be pointed at the same thing.

Both your eyes send signals to your brain. Your brain combines the two views to give you a three-dimensional view of the world.

At least, that's what usually happens. When you try the Hot Dog Finger activity, your brain tries to combine the views of your two eyes—but can't quite manage it. So you end up with a floating hot dog.

3 Do you see a floating hot dog right between your fingertips? Can you make it bigger and smaller? What happens if you wiggle your fingertips? How about if you stick out more fingers?

4 What happens when you close one eye? Try it and see. Open the eye you closed and close the other one. What happens then?

Flipsticks
MAKE-IT-YOURSELF CARTOON KIT
It's easy to make these pictures move!

What Do I Need?

- photocopies of the "Flipstick Cartoons" on pages 44–45
  or
- white paper that you can use for tracing and black marker or dark pencil
- scissors
- bright-colored markers
- clear plastic tape
- file cards
- pencil, straw, or chopstick
- ruler

What Do I Do?

1 If you have a photocopy of pages 44–45, you can skip this step. If you don't, then use a black marker or a dark pencil to trace one set of cartoons onto a piece of paper. Trace the dotted lines, too. Make sure you have a picture *A* and a matching picture *B*.

2 Cut out one set of cartoons—picture *A* and picture *B*. You can color them if you want.

3 Tape each picture to a file card.

4 Turn the first file card over, so the picture is facedown. Put the pencil, straw, or chopstick in the center of the card, about 1 inch from the top, and tape it down. Use plenty of tape. (If you're using a straw, you may want to flatten it a little before you tape it down.)

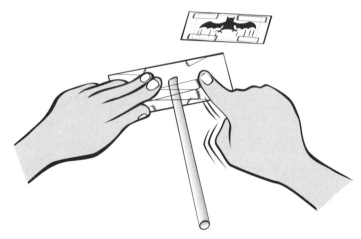

5 Now tape the two cards back to back. Lay the second card over the first, picture side up. Tape the tops and sides of both cards together. Tape the bottom of each card to the pencil. You're going to twirl the pencil, so use plenty of tape—otherwise the cards might fly off.

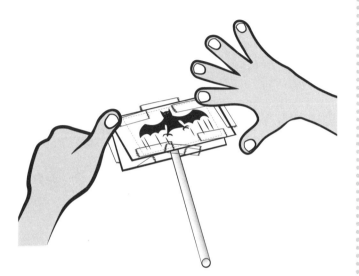

6 Hold the pencil between the palms of your hands and twirl it. The picture changes! (You may need to play around with your twirling to find the best speed. Keep your thumbs flat against your fingers so they don't hit the card when you twirl.)

What's Going On?

Why does your Flipstick work?

When you look at a picture, then quickly flip to another picture, your eye and brain remember the first picture for a fraction of a second, and blend it with the second picture. This visual ability, known as *persistence of vision*, makes the pictures in movies appear to move.

When you watch a movie, the light from the film projector is flickering 72 times a second. Your eye and brain blend the flickering frames of the movie to make a single moving picture.

Wow! I Didn't Know That!

If a light is flashing on and off more than thirty times a second, you see it as a steady light—you don't notice the flickering. When you watch a movie, the screen is dark about half the time. But because the bright picture is flickering seventy-two times a second, you don't even notice the moments of darkness between the pictures.

DRAW YOUR OWN CARTOONS

You can make your own animated cartoons!

What Do I Need?

The same things you used for the Flipsticks (page 40). But instead of photocopying or tracing our cartoons, you can draw your own. You don't need to tape your drawings to file cards—you can draw right on the cards.

What Do I Do?

There are two basic kinds of Flipstick cartoons:

- pictures that add together—like the Man on TV
- pictures that move—like the Jumping Man

Decide which kind you want to draw first, then follow the directions for that kind.

ADD-TOGETHER PICTURES

1 Start by drawing your own Man on TV. Get a blank file card and draw a TV on it using bright-colored markers.

2 Put another blank card down on top of the first one. Make sure the corners of both cards line up. Can you see the TV? If not, hold both cards up to a light or a window.

3 On the second card, draw a man. Make sure that when you hold both cards up to a light, it looks like the man is inside the square of the TV screen.

Now follow steps 4, 5, and 6 on pages 40–41.

With this kind of Flipstick, it's important to:

- be sure that you draw the second picture in the right place—so it lines up with the first picture
- twirl the pencil fast so your eye blends the two pictures together

Ideas to try:

pumpkin/jack-o'-lantern face
fish/fishbowl
bird/cage
sun/clouds

MOVING PICTURES

1 This kind of Flipstick is a little trickier—so start with something simple like a Jumping Man.

On a blank file card, draw a stick man with his arms straight out and his legs pointing down.

2 Put another blank file card on top. Make sure you can see the man. Trace his head and his stick body. *Don't* trace his arms or legs.

Draw the second man's arms pointing up and his legs straight out.

3 Follow steps 4, 5, and 6 on pages 40–41. When you twirl the cards, your man will jump and wave his arms up and down!

With this kind of Flipstick, it's important to:

- trace the parts that are the same in both pictures
- line up the corners of the cards exactly, so the parts that are different will fit
- twirl the pencil so that the picture flips back and forth (if you twirl it too fast, you won't see the picture move)—this part takes a little practice

Ideas to try:

- flapping V
- falling stick

43

Flipstick cartoons

Flipstick cartoons

Read White and Blue

You can read words. You can see colors. Which do you do best?

What Do I Need?

- pencil
- white paper
- six different colors of markers or crayons—we use red, blue, green, brown, purple, and black. (Yellow is hard to read.)
- grown-up

What Do I Do?

You're going to write down the names of the six colors of markers. That's easy. The trick is to write each name in a color that doesn't match it. Then ask a grown-up to read what you've written. Surprise! That may not be so easy.

1 Use the pencil to divide the paper into 3 columns. Divide each column into 6 rectangles. (Don't worry if your rectangles aren't all the same size. You're just making some boxes to write in.) Your paper will look something like this:

2 Use the blue marker. Write the word *red* in one box. Write the word *green* in another box. Write the word *brown* in a third box. Don't put all the blue-colored words next to each other.

3 Now use the red marker. Write the word *blue* in a box. Write *black* in a second box. Write *brown* in a third box.

4 Use each color of marker to write the names of other colors in three boxes. *Don't* write a color's name with the marker of that color. (Don't write *red* with the red marker, or *blue* with the blue marker.) Fill in all the boxes. When you're done, your paper will look something like this, with all the words in different colors:

5 Give the paper to a grown-up. Ask him to read each *word* out loud.

6 Now ask him to read the paper again. But this time, ask him to look at each word and say out loud what *color* it's written in.

7 If you have a watch or a clock, you can time how long it takes the grown-up to read the words and how long it takes him to say the colors. If he's like most people, saying the colors will take a lot longer!

What's Going On?

Why does it take most grown-ups longer to name the colors than to read the words?

Most grown-ups are used to reading words and think that words are very important. As soon as they see a word, they read it. If you ask them to name the color, they still read the word, then realize that's not the task they've been asked to do, and finally name the color. All that wasted mental activity slows them down.

Some grown-ups can name the colors more quickly if the page is upside down. They don't even try to read the upside-down words—so it's easier to name the colors. Of course, that doesn't always work. Members of the Exploratorium's editorial department can read upside down as well as right side up—so they were just as slow when the page was upside down!

My Face Is a Vase!

Turn your very own face into an optical illusion.

What Do I Need?

- chair
- wall
- friend
- lamp
- white paper
- clear plastic tape
- pencil
- scissors
- sheets of colored construction paper

What Do I Do?

1 Put a chair in front of a blank place on a wall. Turn the chair sideways and sit in it.

2 Have your friend shine the light on the side of your face. Ask her to put two sheets of white paper together, one on top of the other, then tape both sheets to the wall so that the shadow of your face—from the top of your head to your chin—fits on the top sheet.

3 Have your friend trace around the shadow of your face—your *silhouette*—with the pencil.

4 Take the papers off the wall. Use the scissors to cut out your silhouette. Cut both sheets of paper at the same time. Don't worry about cutting out the back of the head. Just leave the straight side of the paper.

5 Tape one white face to the edge of a piece of construction paper. Your nose should face the middle of the page.

6 Turn the other white face over and lay it down on the paper so the two faces are nose to nose with about 1 inch between the noses. Do you see the shape of a vase in between your two faces?

Facing Your Friends

This is a fun thing to do at a party. Let everyone have a turn making a silhouette of his or her face—but trace the silhouettes onto different colors of construction paper. When all of the faces are cut out, tape each pair of faces nose to nose on a long sheet of butcher paper or wrapping paper. Then hang the banner on the wall.

7 Move the second face around until the vase is a shape you like. Then tape the second face to the construction paper.

8 When you look at the paper, you can see a vase, or you can see two faces. It's hard to see both things at once. If you want, you can draw some flowers coming out of the vase.

9 Now it's your friend's turn! Ask her to sit in the chair, then do steps 2 and 3 for her. She can do steps 4 to 7 herself.

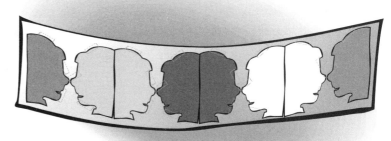

What's Going On?

Why do two faces look like a vase?

The picture that you made with two profiles of your face is a classic optical illusion. When you look at this picture, you need to decide what you should be paying attention to. If you decide that the white shapes are the most important thing in the picture, you see the faces—and the colored construction paper becomes a background. If you decide that the colored shape is the most important, you see a vase—and the white paper becomes a background. You can't see both at once. Psychologists call this type of optical illusion a *figure/ground illusion*.

Wow! I Didn't Know That!

A silhouette is a dark shape seen against a light background. Before there were cameras, people used to have artists make silhouettes of them. The artist cut out a piece of black paper to match the shadow cast by the person's head. The word *silhouette* comes from a Frenchman named Etienne de Silhouette, who cut out black paper portraits as a hobby.

What Else Can I Use to Trick My Eyes?

If you want, you can keep experimenting with optical illusions that trick your eyes and your brain.

Hawk or Goose?

When you taped two silhouettes to a piece of paper, something funny happened. You could see two faces, or you could see a vase in between. But it's really hard to see both things at once. Look at the picture below.

What kind of bird is it? What direction is it flying? Now imagine that it's flying in the other direction. Do you still see the same kind of bird? The picture doesn't change. Your brain just tries to fit it into what you already know about the world. A flying goose has a long neck, and a flying hawk has a long tail.

Letters or numbers?

Look at these symbols.

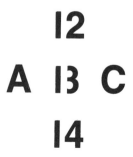

If you read them from left to right, the three symbols are letters— A, B, C. What if you read them from top to bottom? They're numbers — 12, 13, 14. The symbol in the middle doesn't change. Your brain just tries to make it fit into some kind of pattern. If it's in the middle of a pattern of letters, you see it as a letter.

Make your own tricky pictures

Think of some letters and numbers that look alike. A zero and a capital O do. How about a two and a Z? Or a three and a backwards capital E, or a three and a sideways W? Play with letter and number shapes and see what you can come up with.

Think of some things that look similar. A rabbit's ears and a pair of scissors and a duck's bill are sort of the same shape. Could you draw a picture that would look like both a duck and a rabbit?

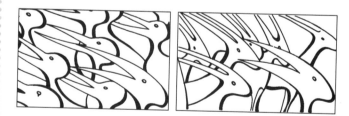

Is the figure in the lower right of each picture a bird or an antelope?

Rings, Wings, and Other Flying Things

On November 18, 1995, John Collins stood on the floor of the Exploratorium holding a piece of tissue paper he had folded into a flyer called the Tumble Wing. When he threw the Tumble Wing, a timer began counting off the seconds. The world's record for the longest flight of a hand-launched paper aircraft was 18.8 seconds. Would the Tumble Wing break the record? Yes! It stayed in the air for almost twice that long—32.39 seconds.

John Collins works as a TV news director, but for the last twenty-five years, his hobby has been making paper airplanes. In his book *Return to the Fold,* John says, "The simple act of creating a toy—a flying toy, at that—from a castaway piece of material has always appealed to me. The paper world is confined only by imagination. A piece of paper is the original multimedia. A virtual toy chest can be created with scratch paper and folding."

If you want to design your own planes, John's advice is to just keep folding. Doodle in 3-D. Each time you make a fold, be sure it's crisp and sharp. If you try something new, take notes or make a drawing so you can make the same fold again. Experiment with different kinds of paper—recycled copier paper, tissue paper, even pages from the phone book. Paper that's been run through a copier is really good for most planes because it's been stiffened by the heat and been given a very thin coating of plastic that makes it a little stronger.

All the planes in John's books are made from a single sheet of folded paper, without scissors or glue. In this chapter, you can find out how to make four different flying things from other kinds of stuff, too.

With a scrap of patterned tissue paper the size of a chewing gum wrapper, paper-airplane maker John Collins set a world record. His tiny plane stayed aloft for 32.39 seconds, breaking the previous record of 18.8 seconds.

Some funny-looking planes can fly really well!

Spinning Blimps

Become an aircraft designer—with scissors and paper.

What Do I Need?

- paper
- ruler
- scissors
- crayons or markers (if you want)

What Do I Do?

1 Cut a strip of paper about 6 to 8 inches long and ½ inch wide.

2 Cut halfway across the strip about ½ inch from one end. Turn the strip around and do the same thing on the other end. You'll end up with a strip that looks like this:

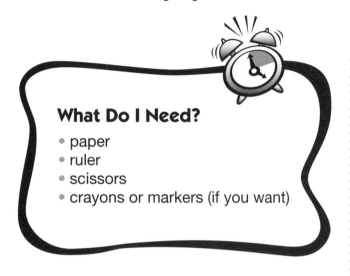

3 Slip the slot at one end into the slot at the other end. You'll make something that looks like a little fish.

4 That's it! You've made a Spinning Blimp. Hold the blimp high over your head and drop it. It'll spin like mad on its way to the ground.

My blimp spins best when I hold it so that the fish looks like it's swimming on its side.

Wow! I Didn't Know That!

Alexander Graham Bell—the inventor of the telephone—believed that in the future, giant kites would carry people from place to place.

5 Now you have a blimp that spins through the air. It's really simple to make more blimps and experiment with changes in the basic blimp design. See if you can make a blimp that spins faster or stays up for a longer time.

It's best if you make just one change at a time. Here are some things you can try:

- Make the paper strip longer or shorter.
- Make the paper strip wider or narrower.
- Make the tails longer or shorter.
- Cut the ends of the tails so they're pointy.
- Try using different kinds of paper.

The Exploratorium's Home Scientists enjoyed experimenting with Spinning Blimps. The Hollister family discovered that pinching the blimp's nose to make it pointed made the blimp spin faster and better. The Morgan family noticed that the higher above the ground they held their Spinning Blimps, the better the blimps worked—which gave tall people an advantage. And the Werner family made their own "Blimp-o-Maniac" form to record the results of their blimp experiments.

6 You can also color your paper strip before you fold it into a blimp. That won't make it spin better, but it's fun to watch patterns and colors spin through the air.

What's Going On?

Learning to experiment

The Spinning Blimp is a great toy to experiment with. Change a little something and see what happens. Your blimp probably flies fine—but maybe a blimp with a shorter tail would spin even better. We've suggested some ways to modify your blimp, but our suggestions are just the beginning. What other modifications can you and your kids come up with?

While you're experimenting, it may look like you're just fooling around. And you *are* fooling around—but you're also paying attention to what happens when you change your blimp. By making changes and noticing what happens, you're following in the footsteps of many scientists. Many scientific discoveries have come about because someone was "just fooling around."

When you're fooling around, some of the things you try won't work very well. Maybe you make a change in your Spinning Blimp and it takes a nosedive. That's okay. In fact, that's great. You've learned something about what doesn't work, which is important to know. And maybe sometime you'll *want* to make a blimp that dives—and you'll know how.

Another part of fooling around scientifically is keeping track of your results. What works well? What doesn't work at all? Keep track of experiments that you try. If you come up with a new design that you like, tell us about it. We'd like to try it, too!

Roto-Copter

This simple paper toy spins through the air like a mini-helicopter.

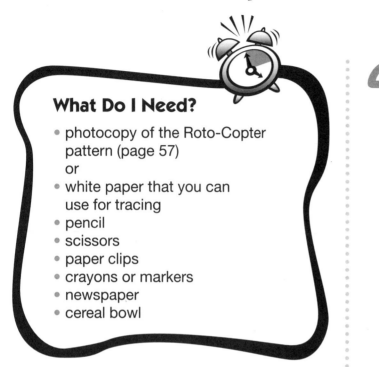

What Do I Need?

- photocopy of the Roto-Copter pattern (page 57)
  or
- white paper that you can use for tracing
- pencil
- scissors
- paper clips
- crayons or markers
- newspaper
- cereal bowl

What Do I Do?

1 If you have a photocopy of the Roto-Copter pattern, you can skip this step. If you don't, then trace the Roto-Copter pattern onto a piece of paper.

2 Cut along the solid lines only. Fold on the dotted lines.

3 Fold *A* toward you. Fold *B* away from you.

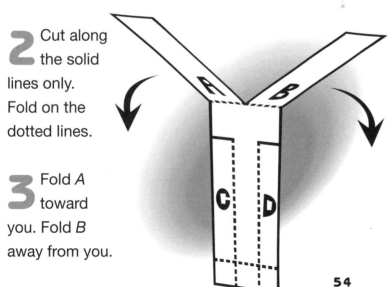

4 Fold *C* and *D* over each other so they overlap.

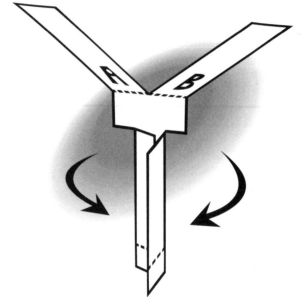

5 Fold the bottom up and put a paper clip on it.

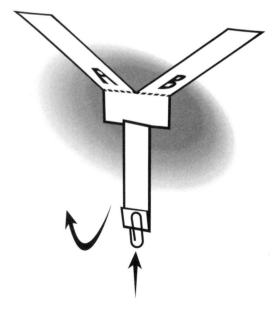

54

6 Hold the Roto-Copter by the paper clip. Throw it like a baseball, as high and far as you can. It will spin to the floor. You can also stand on a chair or on the stairs and drop it. Ask a grown-up if you can drop it out the window.

7 If you want, you can use crayons or markers to color your Roto-Copter before you fold it. The colors will blur together when it spins.

Wow! I Didn't Know That!

Igor Sikorsky designed the first successful helicopter in the late 1930s. His inspiration came from drawings of an aircraft with a spinning wing, drawn by Leonardo da Vinci nearly five hundred years before.

ROTO-TARGET

Make three Roto-Copters for each person. Use a marker to draw a 1-foot circle on a piece of newspaper. Put a cereal bowl in the middle of the circle. The circle is the target area and the bowl is the bull's-eye. Take turns standing on a chair at the edge of the newspaper and dropping your Roto-Copters. At the Exploratorium, we get 3 points for a bull's-eye, 2 points for a copter inside the circle, and one point for just hitting the newspaper—but you can make up any rules you want.

The Home Scientists in the Gee family tested different types of paper and discovered that stiff paper (like the paper in a manila folder) made the best Roto-Coptors. And the Werner family found that maple seeds from the tree in their front yard spun just like their Roto-Coptors.

What's Going On?

Why does the Roto-Copter spin?

When the Roto-Copter falls, air pushes up against the blades, bending them up just a little. When air pushes upward on the slanted blade, some of that thrust becomes a sideways, or horizontal, push.

Why doesn't the copter simply move sideways through the air? That's because there are two blades, each getting the same push, but in opposite directions. The two opposing thrusts work together to cause the toy to spin.

Next time you drop your copter, notice which direction it spins as it falls. Is it clockwise or counterclockwise? Now bend the blades in opposite directions—if blade *A* was bent toward you and blade *B* was bent away, bend *B* toward you and *A* away. Drop the copter again. Now which way does it spin?

In the Spinning Blimp, air pushes up on the flat sides of the strip of paper. When the flat side of the paper strip is parallel to the ground, the blimp drifts down like a flat piece of paper. But if the blimp tilts so that the flat side of the strip is at an angle to the ground, the paper strip gets a sideways push, just like the blade of the copter, sending the blimp spinning. Each time the flat strip comes around, it gets another push and goes for another spin.

As the copter falls, air collides with the blade and is forced outward. This outward movement causes a push on the copter that makes it spin.

ROTO-COPTER PATTERNS

Does a big Roto-Copter spin differently than a little one? Here are two sizes for you to try.

Trace or photocopy

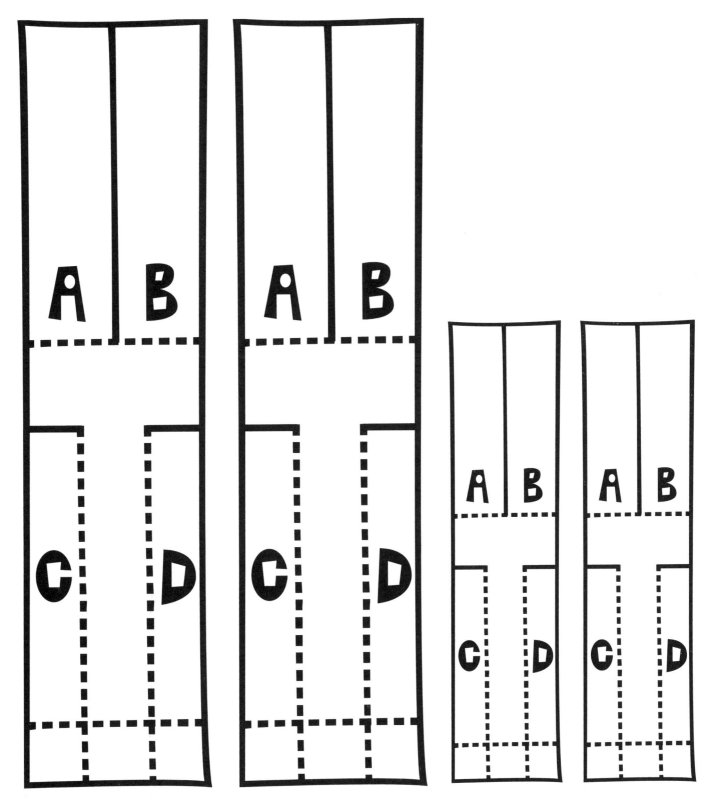

Fabulous Foam Flyer (The F-3)

You can use a foam tray to make a super glider.

What Do I Need?

- Styrofoam tray from your supermarket (ask at the meat or bakery counter for a clean, unused tray)
- marker
- ruler
- scissors
- clear plastic tape
- paper clips

What Do I Do?

1 On the flat part of the tray, measure and draw a square that's 4 or 5 inches on each side. Cut out the square.

2 Measure to the middle of one side of the square and make a dot. Draw lines from the dot to each of the opposite corners to make a triangle.

Cut along the lines you drew. You'll have one big triangle and two little ones.

MIDDLE

3 The big triangle is the wing. Measure to the middle of the bottom of the wing and make a dot. Cut a slot from this dot to the center of the wing and pop the little strip of foam out. How thick is your piece of foam? That's how wide the slot should be.

4 One of the little triangles is the rudder. Cut a slot in it that's the same size as the one in the big triangle. Cut off the pointy end so it looks like the picture. (Keep the other little triangle as a spare.)

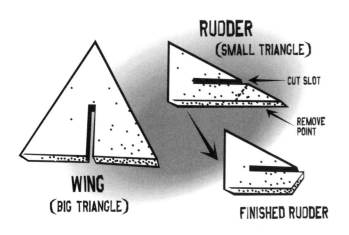

RUDDER
(SMALL TRIANGLE)

CUT SLOT

REMOVE POINT

WING
(BIG TRIANGLE)

FINISHED RUDDER

5 Push the rudder onto the wing so the two slots fit together. If it feels loose, you can tape the rudder to the wing. The rudder will stick out a little from the back of the wing.

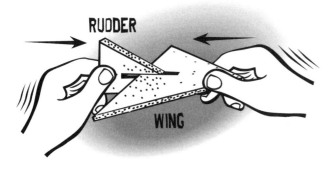

RUDDER

WING

6 Now you can see if it flies. Hold the F-3 by the bottom part of the rudder and throw it forward.

7 If your F-3 just wobbles and falls to the floor, it needs more weight in its nose. (The nose is the front point of the wing.) Push a paper clip onto the nose. Now how does your F-3 fly?

Once you've made your F-3, it's great to fly it outside.

Exploratorium Home Scientist Matthew Smidebush made an F-3 from a tray that had bumps on one side. He discovered that the bumpy F-3 flew better than ones he made from smooth trays.

Can You Make Your F-3 Fly Better?

Scientists figure out how to make things better by *trial and error.* That means you try something, then you see what happens.

Let's say you want to make an F-3 that flies farther. First you need to know how far your F-3 flies just as it is. Throw it three times and write down how far it goes each time. (Use your own feet to measure—see how many steps it is from the start to where the F-3 landed.)

Now make a change and try again. Some changes will make it fly farther. Some won't. Some changes may even make it crash. That's okay. You can learn just as much from mistakes as you can from things that work.

It's important to change only one thing at a time, then see what happens. Too many changes are too confusing. It's also good to write down what you've tried.

Here are some things to try. You can also try anything else you think will work.

- Put more weight (paper clips, pennies, etc.) on the nose.
- Put weight on the back or the sides of the wing, or on the rudder.
- Make little rudders from the leftover foam and put them on either side of the big rudder.
- If you have more foam trays, make an F-3 that's bigger or smaller than the first. Almost any size will work—just be sure you start with a square!

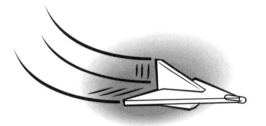

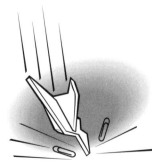

What's Going On?

Tips for parents

To preserve family harmony, Home Scientist Doug Grumann suggests that you avoid running out of materials. "Start with a lot of Styrofoam trays," he advises. He also recommends that you don't force your kids to be too scientific with their variations. His kids liked to change a lot of things every time. Kids may start out experimenting that way—and later on become more methodical in their modifications.

Why do these toys fly?

The same principles are at work in all of your flyers. Gravity is pulling them down, but at the same time, air helps hold them up.

If you drop a flat sheet of paper, it flutters to the ground, wobbling this way and that. To reach the ground, the paper has to push the air aside. Each time the paper wobbles, it lets more air flow past it, and it gets a little closer to the ground. Since a flat sheet of paper has to push a lot of air out of the way, it falls slowly.

Crumple that same piece of paper into a ball, and it will fall straight down without fluttering. The ball of paper has the same weight as before, but air can flow around it easily and it falls quickly.

For something to glide through the air (like the F-3 or any other flying toy), there must be a balance between the gravity that's pulling the glider down and the air resistance that's helping to hold it up. You need to balance these forces so that the glider moves forward, propelled by the pull of gravity.

Why does a paper clip help the F-3 fly better?

Adding a paper clip to your F-3 changes the glider's center of gravity. The center of gravity is the glider's balance point. Put a support under this spot and the plane will balance perfectly.

How well the F-3 flies also depends on the location of the glider's center of pressure. Suppose you had your F-3 in a blast of air, pushing it upward. Suppose you wanted to push down on the plane in just one spot to keep the air from pushing it up. The place where you push down is the center of pressure.

For a glider to move smoothly through the air, the center of gravity needs to be in front of the center of pressure. Then gravity will pull the front of the glider downward and the air beneath the wings will keep it from falling right to the ground. Instead the glider slides smoothly through the air.

Take a look at your F-3. The center of pressure is toward the back of the plane, where the wings spread out. The broad wings, like a flat sheet of paper, block the air and keep the glider from falling straight down.

center of pressure

center of gravity

What does the rudder on the F-3 do?

The F-3's rudder, the triangle that's perpendicular to the wing, keeps the glider from sliding through the air sideways. The rudder ensures that the plane's nose is always pointing in the direction that it's flying. Of course, if you bend the rudder, you can change the direction that the plane is flying. By changing the angle of the rudder (or by gently bending the back of the wings up or down), you can change the way the air flows over the rudder and wing and push the plane out of a straight path.

Hoopster

Most paper airplanes are flat, but these paper hoops can really fly!

> Hoopsters fly best outdoors on a day that's not too windy.

What Do I Need?

- scissors
- ruler
- 3-x-5-inch file cards (or a file folder or some other stiff paper)
- clear plastic tape
- plastic straws (not the kind that bend)

What Do I Do?

1 Cut a file card the long way into three equal strips. If you're using stiff paper, make three strips that are 1 inch wide and 5 inches long.

2 Put a piece of tape on the end of one strip. Curl the paper into a little hoop and tape the ends together.

SMALL HOOP

3 Put the other two strips end to end, so they overlap a little. Tape them together to make one long strip, and put another piece of tape on one end. Curl the strip into a hoop and tape the ends together.

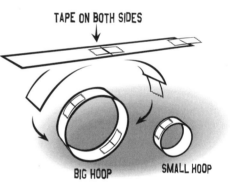

TAPE ON BOTH SIDES

BIG HOOP   SMALL HOOP

4 Put one end of a straw onto the middle of a strip of tape. Put the big hoop on top of the straw and fold the tape up the sides of the hoop.

5 This part can be a little tricky. Put another strip of tape at the other end of the straw.
Press the small hoop very gently onto the tape. Move it around until it lines up with the big hoop, then press the tape down firmly.

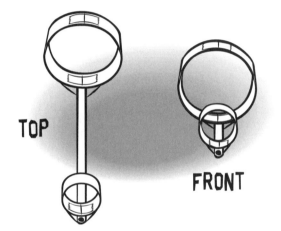

TOP

FRONT

6 Now comes the fun! Hold the Hoopster in the middle of the straw, with the little hoop in front. Throw it like a spear. It may take a little practice, but once you get the hang of it, your Hoopster will really fly!

7 If you want to experiment with Hoopsters, here are some other things you can try:

• Put a paper clip at the bottom of the small hoop.
• Make a really long Hoopster with two straws. Cut a little slit at the end of one straw and pinch it so it fits inside the other straw, then tape them together.
• Make a double Hoopster with two little hoops side by side on one end and two big hoops side by side on the other. (You'll need two file cards.)

Our Home Scientists were surprised that their Hoopsters flew. The Graff family wondered how anything that looked so awkward could fly at all! Kids in the Popka family spent days developing new designs for their Hoopsters—including one that was 7 feet long! And the kids in the Hino family got out the butterfly net and tried to catch the Hoopsters as they flew by!

What Else Can I Do with My Flying Things?

Now that you've made four very different kinds of flying things, you can keep exploring and experimenting with ways to make them spin, glide, or soar even better.

What Do You Want to Do?

That's the first thing you need to decide. Do you want to make a Roto-Copter that spins faster? Or a Hoopster that goes twice as far?

See What Works—and What Doesn't

You've watched how all your planes fly, and you've probably watched them crash, too. Maybe you taped a penny to your Roto-Copter, and it fell like a rock. That's great. You found out that a little weight may be a good thing, but too much weight may not. Make a change, then watch to see how that one little thing affects the way your plane flies.

Fly with a Friend

Sometimes you may get stuck. You've tried everything you can think of, and your F-3 or your Hoopster still won't do what you want. That's when it's good to get another brain involved. If you make some flying things with a friend, chances are he or she will make one just a little different from yours. If you share your ideas, you can save a lot of time and frustration.

Share Your Success

If you design a terrific new plane, let us know. Send a sample plane or a detailed drawing to the Exploratorium. We'll try to make one ourselves, and we'll tell other people about it so that they can play with your invention!

Dramatic Static

Have you ever touched a doorknob and gotten a shock? That shock is *static electricity,* the same thing that makes lightning flash and makes your socks stick together in the dryer.

Back in the 1750s, no one had a dryer. Or electric lights. Some people had found that they could make sparks by rubbing an amber bead with a piece of fur. But most people thought that electricity was just a parlor trick, a way to amuse people.

Benjamin Franklin disagreed. He spent a lot of time experimenting with electricity, learning about the sparks and how they behaved. He noticed that the sparks looked like tiny bolts of lightning. To prove that lightning and electricity were the same thing, he tied a metal key to a kite string, then flew his kite in a thunderstorm. When he touched his knuckle to the key, he felt a spark.

That was a *very* dangerous thing to do. The next person to try this experiment was electrocuted! When Franklin realized how powerful electricity was, he experimented with ways to keep people safe during lightning storms. In 1752, he invented the lightning rod—a tall metal pole stuck deep into the ground. Lightning hit the pole and traveled harmlessly into the ground, instead of hitting the house. Thousands of people bought "Franklin rods" for their houses and began taking electricity seriously.

Ben Franklin's first experiments were very simple—he rubbed things together to make sparks. That's something you can do, too. Out of his experiments came the science of electricity and, eventually, the dryer where your socks may stick together.

> You can do some shocking experiments with an ordinary balloon!

Lightning bolts are the world's biggest sparks of static electricity! This photo shows a lightning storm at Kitt Peak National Observatory, southwest of Tucson, Arizona.

Jumping Pepper

You can make pepper jump without touching it!

What Do I Need?

- a dry day
- someplace where there's no wind
- salt and pepper
- something plastic—like a square of Saran Wrap, the plastic lid from a margarine tub, a plastic straw, a plastic comb, a plastic spoon, or an inflated balloon
- a clean head of hair or a wool sweater

What Do I Do?

1 Do this on a dry day, in a place where there's no wind, like a room with the windows closed. Make a little pile of salt and pepper on a table.

2 Rub the piece of plastic on your hair or on a wool sweater. (You can also rub the plastic on a dog or a cat, if you have one handy.)

3 Hold the piece of plastic just a few inches above the pile of salt and pepper. If you're using Saran Wrap, stretch it between your hands and hold it flat. The pepper will jump up and stick to the plastic.

4 If your pepper doesn't jump, try holding the plastic closer to the pepper. If it *still* doesn't jump, try rubbing the plastic on a different sweater or on someone else's hair. If the pepper still won't jump, try a different piece of plastic. (Some plastics work better than others.) If all else fails, try again on a different day.

5 If you use a plastic lid or Saran Wrap, you'll hear something that sounds like rain as the pepper slams into the plastic. If you hold the plastic close enough, you may be able to get the salt jumping, too.

What's Going On?

Tips for parents

This experiment works best on dry days. On humid days, when the air is moist, it's harder for plastic to hold on to a static charge.

You can try this experiment at your own kitchen table or in a fast-food restaurant with a plastic straw or a plastic spoon. You need to be somewhere where there's no wind, since a breeze will blow away all your pepper.

This experiment works best with clean hair. One mother commented that experimenting with static gave her kids an incentive to bathe frequently, since they needed clean hair to create a static charge. Be aware that hair conditioner, hair spray, and other hair goop may interfere with your experiment.

Why does the pepper jump?

Like everything else in your house, the plastic that you rubbed on your hair is made of tiny particles called *atoms*. Atoms are made of even tinier particles called *electrons*, *protons*, and *neutrons*. These subatomic particles make the pepper jump, make clothes stick together in the dryer, and make lightning flash.

When you rub the plastic on your hair, you are pulling some atoms to pieces. You're yanking electrons off your hair and sticking them to the plastic. Usually, an atom has just as many electrons as it has protons. But after you're done rubbing, your hair has fewer electrons than protons and the plastic has more electrons than protons.

Electrons and protons are both electrically charged particles. Electrons are negatively charged, and protons are positively charged. Negative charges attract positive charges, so electrons attract protons. That's one reason that protons and electrons stick together to form atoms—the attraction between the oppositely charged particles. At the same time, negative charges push away other negative charges, so electrons push away other electrons.

When you rub plastic on your hair, you add electrons to the plastic. By piling all those extra electrons in one place and leaving the protons behind, you're building up an electric charge. When you hold your piece of plastic over the pepper, the electrons that you've crowded together on the plastic push away the electrons in the pepper and attract the protons. The pull of the attraction overcomes the push, and the pepper jumps up to join the electrons on the plastic.

You can build up a static charge by rubbing plastic on your own hair, on a wool sweater, or on the fur of a family pet. The Home Scientists in the Pankow family commented that their dogs liked their special backrubs. In the Dunn family, eight-year-old Joel got tired of rubbing a balloon on his hair. According to his mother, "his face lit up when he saw his thirteen-year-old brother's hairy legs. Joel ran toward him yelling, 'Give me some static, Jason!' Joel got some static, but not the kind he wanted!"

Remote Control Roller

Rub a balloon on your head, then watch a soda can race across the floor!

What Do I Need?

- empty soda can
- blown-up balloon
- your hair

What Do I Do?

1 Put the can on its side on a table or the floor—anyplace that's flat and smooth. Hold it with your finger until it stays still.

2 Rub the balloon back and forth on your hair really fast.

3 Hold the balloon about an inch in front of the can. The can will start to roll, even though you're not touching it!

4 Move the balloon away from the can—slowly—and the can will follow the balloon.

5 If you move the balloon to the other side of the can, the can will roll in the other direction.

6 How fast will the can roll? How far can you roll it before the can stops? Will it roll uphill?

7 If you have some friends with cans and balloons, you can have a race across the room or down the sidewalk.

68

Rub a Balloon on Your Head and You Can . . .

Bend Water

Turn on the faucet in your bathroom or kitchen. Don't run the water too hard, but more than a little trickle. Now rub a balloon on your head and hold the balloon near the water. The stream of water will bend toward the balloon!

Give Yourself Funny Hair

Rub the balloon on your head, then pull it away. Your hair will stick out and look really funny. (This can also happen when you comb your hair with a plastic comb.) What if you hold the balloon near your arm? Can you feel the hairs on your arm move? Will it work on doll hair? How about animal fur?

Wow! I Didn't Know That!

A Xerox machine uses static electricity to make copies. When you rub a balloon on your head, the balloon is charged with electricity. Inside a Xerox machine is a plastic drum that is also charged. When you put a piece of paper on the glass, a copy of it goes onto the drum. Where there were dark places on the paper, the static charge on the drum attracts the black plastic toner powder. Then the powdered places go onto a blank piece of paper, and the paper is heated. The toner melts and makes black letters on the new piece of paper.

Stick the Balloon to Your Face!

Once you've rubbed the balloon on your head, it will stick to other things—with no glue. You can stick it to the wall, to the TV, or even to your face.

What's Going On?

Why does the soda can roll?

Remote Control Roller is a lot like Jumping Pepper. Basically, you pile up electrons on one thing and use them to attract the protons in something else. When you rub a balloon on your hair, it ends up loaded with electrons. Those electrons can attract the protons in a soda can, the protons in a trickle of water, the protons in your hair, or the protons in a wall.

Why do clothes stick together in the dryer?

The attraction between protons and electrons can also make clothes stick together in the dryer. When you dry clothes in the dryer, different fabrics rub together, and electrons from a cotton sock (for instance) may rub off onto a polyester shirt. That's why clothes sometimes stick together and make sparks when you pull them apart.

You may have used antistatic sheets in your dryer. As these sheets bounce around with your clothes, they add a uniform antistatic coating to the fabric. Rather than cotton rubbing against polyester, you've got the antistatic coating on the cotton rubbing against the antistatic coating on the polyester. No electrons rub off—and you don't get any static cling.

Super Sparker

Make very, very, very tiny lightning, anytime you want!

What Do I Need?

- scissors
- Styrofoam tray from your supermarket (ask at the meat or bakery counter for a clean, unused tray)
- masking tape
- aluminum pie tin

What Do I Do?

1 Cut a piece off one corner of the Styrofoam tray, as the picture shows. You'll have a long bent piece that looks a little like a hockey stick.

2 Tape the bent piece to the center of the pie tin. Now you have a handle!

3 Rub the bottom of the Styrofoam tray on your hair. Rub it all over, really fast.

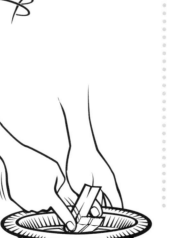

4 Put the tray upside down on a table or on the floor.

5 Use the handle to pick up the pie tin. Hold it about a foot over the Styrofoam tray and drop it.

6 Now—very slowly—touch the tip of your finger to the pie tin. Wow! What a spark! (Be careful. DON'T touch the Styrofoam tray. If you do, you won't get a spark.)

7 Use the handle to pick up the pie tin again. Touch the tin with the tip of your finger. Wow! Another great spark.

8 Drop the pie tin onto the Styrofoam tray again. Touch the pie tin. Another spark! Use the handle to pick up the pie tin. More sparks!

9 You can do this over and over for a long time. If the pie tin stops giving you a spark, just rub the Styrofoam tray on your head again, and start over.

Sparks in the Dark

Try using your Super Sparker in the dark. Can you see the tiny lightning bolts you make? What color are they?

What's Going On?

What makes the Super Sparker spark?

When you rub Styrofoam on your hair, you pull electrons off your hair and pile them up on the Styrofoam. When you put an aluminum pie tin on the Styrofoam, the electrons on the Styrofoam pull on the protons in the pie tin—and they also push on the electrons. Some of the electrons in metals are *free electrons*—they can move around inside the metal. These free electrons try to move as far away from the Styrofoam as they can. When you touch the pie tin, those free electrons leap to your hand, making a spark.

After the electrons jump to your hand, the pie tin is short some electrons. When you lift the pie tin away from the Styrofoam plate, you've got a pie tin that attracts any and all nearby electrons. If you hold your finger close to the metal, electrons jump from your finger back to the pie tin, making another spark.

When you put the pie tin back on the Styrofoam plate, you start the whole process over again.

What does all this have to do with lightning?

The lightning bolt is a dramatic example of static electricity in action. You see lightning when a spark of moving electrons races up or down between a cloud and the ground (or between two clouds). The moving electrons bump into air molecules along the way, heating them to a temperature five times hotter than the surface of the sun. This hot air expands as a supersonic shock wave, then turns into a regular sound wave, which you hear as thunder.

What Else Can I Do with Static Electricity?

Your house is filled with things that will make static electricity. See if you can find a few— and use them in your own experiments.

Wiggle Your Beans

Using static electricity, you can make tiny things jump or stand up and dance.

Get some tiny things—like rice, dried beans, or paper torn into little pieces. Rub a balloon on your head, then hold it above the tiny things. Scraps of paper will jump up and stick to the balloon. Beans are heavier, and they'll just wiggle around. Move the balloon back and forth to make the beans dance.

Can you find five more things in your house that will dance or jump? You'll have to test each one to see if it works. When you do that, you're experimenting like a scientist.

Rub This on Your Head

A balloon isn't the only thing that will make your paper jump. Rub a plastic comb on your hair. Does that work? What about a pencil? The lid from a margarine tub?

Try other things you have around the house. Some may work great, but some may not work at all. Can you find three more things that you can rub on your hair and then use to make the paper jump?

Give Your Head a Rest

Now you've got lots of things that you can rub on your hair and use to make the paper jump. But what if you didn't have any hair? Some people don't. Is there anything else you can use for rubbing?

Start with a balloon or something else that you know will work. But instead of rubbing it on your hair, try rubbing it on a wool sweater. Or on your dog's fur. Or maybe on a cotton T-shirt or a nylon sock.

Do any of those work? What else can you find that will work?

MARVELOUS MUSIC AND ASTOUNDING SOUNDS

At the Exploratorium, we know lots of people who like to experiment with sound. Some of these people call themselves scientists. Some call themselves musicians.

It doesn't really matter what you call yourself—if you want to experiment with interesting sounds, building musical instruments is a great way to do it.

Thousands of years ago, people started making musical instruments out of stuff they found in the world around them. They made drums from hollow logs, flutes from bamboo sticks, rattles from empty gourds, and trumpets from conch shells.

People are still inventing new musical instruments. Back in the 1930s, someone on the Caribbean island of Trinidad got a good loud sound by whacking an empty oil barrel with a stick. Then he figured out how to change the oil barrel to make a better sound. He cut one end off the barrel and hammered down the other end to make a bowl. He cut grooves in the metal bowl and found out that he got a different sound when he hit each different part of the bowl. After much experimenting—by that unknown inventor and other people who were interested in musical sounds—the people of Trinidad had an instrument that's now known all over the world as a steel drum. Today, the music of Trinidad—a style of music known as calypso—is filled with the beautiful bell-like tones of the steel drum.

> Build your own musical instruments—and make a band to play your own kind of music.

On the island of Trinidad, people turn big steel oil barrels into musical instruments known as steel drums. Kenny Charles and Elizabeth La Mantia Scott play steel drums for the Exploratorium's Steel Band Jamboree.

Straw Oboe

Make a musical duck call from a drinking straw.

Playing an oboe made from a drinking straw isn't always easy. You may need a grown-up's help.

What Do I Need?

- a few plastic drinking straws
- scissors
- a little patience

What Do I Do?

1 With your fingers, flatten one end of the straw. If it's tough plastic, it won't stay flat easily. You can slide it between your front teeth to make a sharp crease in the plastic.

2 With the scissors, cut the flattened end of the straw so that it looks like this:

3 Put the end that you cut into your mouth and blow. If you're lucky, you'll get a sound right away.

4 If you don't get a sound, try pinching the straw between your teeth as you blow. (Don't pinch so hard you close off the straw, just flatten it a little.) You can also use your fingers to squeeze the straw flat at your lips. If you still don't get a sound, try blowing a little harder—or maybe a little softer.

5 Sometimes a Straw Oboe will work on your first try. Sometimes you have to start over with a new straw. It's tricky, but keep trying and sooner or later you'll get a buzzing, humming sound, like a musical duck call.

6 Once you've made a Straw Oboe, you can experiment to change the sound it makes. Try cutting off the end of the straw. Does the length of the oboe change the note it plays? Snip little holes in a long oboe. If you use your fingers to cover and uncover the holes as you play, you can make different notes.

7 Ken Finn, who works at the Exploratorium, made a Straw Trombone using a straw with a slightly bigger diameter than his Straw Oboe. He slid the second straw over the Straw Oboe and changed its pitch by sliding the second straw to make the tube longer or shorter.

Can you come up with any other ways to change the sound your Straw Oboe makes?

What's Going On?

Where does the buzzing sound come from?

Touch your hand to the front of your throat and say something. You'll not only hear the sound of your voice—you'll also feel it in your fingers. Sound—whether it's the sound of your own voice, the buzzing of the Straw Oboe, or the ringing of a bell—begins with a vibration.

In the Straw Oboe, you can feel the vibrations against your lips. Two parts of the straw are vibrating like the reeds in an oboe. As you build the musical instruments in this chapter, you may want to try to figure out what's vibrating to make each sound.

People often describe sounds as high-pitched or low-pitched. The screech of a whistling teakettle or the jingling of a tiny bell is high-pitched. The rumble of a bass drum or the ringing of the big bell in a clock tower is low-pitched.

Short Straw Oboes play high-pitched notes, and longer Straw Oboes play low-pitched notes. By changing the length of the instrument, you can change the pitch of the note it plays.

Rain Sticks

Listen to the sound of a rainstorm—anywhere, anytime!

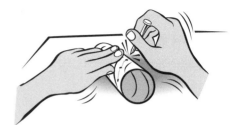

What Do I Need?

- cardboard tube (A paper towel roll is okay, but a long tube from gift-wrapping paper is even better. You can also take two or three paper towel rolls and tape them together.)
- marker
- ruler
either:
- sixty 1-inch nails
or
- a 1-inch nail and sixty round toothpicks
- tape (masking tape or packing tape is good)
- paper
- rice or small beans (uncooked!)

What Do I Do?

1 Paper tubes are made in a spiral. Use a marker to draw dots about half an inch apart, all the way down the spiral seam of the tube.

2 Ask a grown-up to use a nail to poke a hole at each dot.

3 If you have enough nails, poke a nail all the way in at each dot. (Make sure the nails don't poke through the other side of the tube.) You'll need about 30 nails for each paper towel tube.

or

If you don't have that many nails, or your nails are too long, use round toothpicks. Break the toothpicks in half, and poke one of them partway into each hole. Leave just a little nub sticking out.

4 Wrap tape around the tube to hold the nails or toothpicks in place, so they don't fall out when you

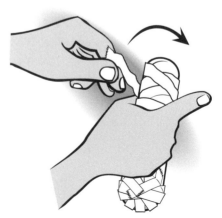

5 Cut two circles of paper just a little bigger than the ends of the tube. Put one circle over one end of the tube. Cover the circle with tape so the whole end of the tube is sealed shut.

6 Put a handful of rice or beans into the open end of the tube. Cover the open end with your hand, and turn the tube over. Add more rice (or beans) until you like the sound. Beans will make a hard sound, and rice will make a softer sound.

7 Put the second circle of paper over the open end of the tube, and seal that end shut with tape.

8 Now you can hear the sound of rain anytime you want. Just turn your Rain Stick over and listen. When the sound tops, turn it over again!

When I turn over my Rain Stick, I can feel the tube vibrating. That's what makes the sound I hear!

Wow! I Didn't Know That!

Rain sticks come from Chile. The people in Chile make them from cactus. The thorns are pulled off and pushed back in through the soft flesh of the cactus. Then the cactus is left out in the sun to dry—with the thorns on the inside. Later the hollow cactus is filled with small pebbles, and the ends are sealed with pieces of wood.

The Tingler

This simple whistle makes some surprising noises!

What Do I Need?

- scissors
- corrugated cardboard
- ruler
- masking tape
- clear tape

What Do I Do?

1 Cut two pieces of cardboard about 3 inches long and an inch wide. Make sure the two pieces are the same size.

2 Fold a piece of masking tape over the long sides of each piece of cardboard. (This keeps the cardboard from getting really soggy when you put it in your mouth.)

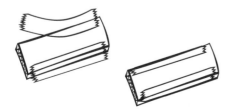

3 Take about a foot of masking tape, and wrap it around (and around and around) one end of one of the cardboard pieces. It should wrap around four or five times.

4 Repeat step 3 until you have wrapped both ends of both pieces of cardboard. The tape will make the ends thicker than the middle.

5 Cut two pieces of clear tape just a little shorter than your piece of cardboard. Put the sticky sides of the tape together to make a strip of clear plastic.

6 Use the masking tape to tape one end of the plastic strip to the end of one piece of card-board. Stretch the strip tight, then tape the other end down. (Don't stretch it so tight that the cardboard bends.)

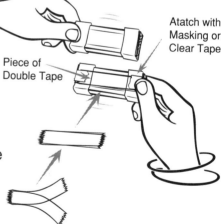

Atatch with Masking or Clear Tape

Piece of Double Tape

7 Put the other piece of cardboard on top. Now you have a cardboard sandwich with a strip of plastic in the middle.

8 Play your Tingler like a harmonica. Hold the taped ends of the cardboard together tightly, and blow through the middle. Don't squeeze the middle part. If you get a whistle (or a hum or buzz)—that's great. Wrap a piece of tape around each end of the cardboard to tape the "sandwich" together.

9 If you don't get a good noise, untape the plastic strip and pull it a little tighter. Move it around until you like the sound it makes, then tape everything together.

10 Now play with your Tingler. What kind of sound do you get if you blow really hard? If you tighten your lips? If you wiggle the cardboard? If you bend it a little?

Advanced Tingler

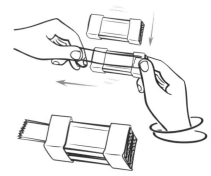

You can control the sound of your Tingler by changing the design just a little.

- Steps 1 to 4 are the same.
- In step 5, cut two pieces of tape *longer* than the cardboard, and stick them together to make a plastic strip.
- Tape one end of the strip down, and let the other end hang out like a tail.
  - Put the two pieces of cardboard on top of each other. Now you have a sandwich with a tail. Tape around the ends so that the two pieces are held loosely together, but the tail can still move.
- Blow through the middle of the Tingler. Pull on the plastic tail to make the sound change.

What's Going On?

Why does the sound of the Advanced Tingler change when I pull the strip?

In the Tingler, air from your mouth starts the strip of tape vibrating, which makes the buzzing sound you hear. In the Advanced Tingler, you can change the sound by pulling the strip of tape tight or letting it be loose. The tighter the strip, the faster it vibrates—and the higher the pitch of the sound.

Wow! I Didn't Know That!

In Rajasthan—a state in the northern part of India—a whistle like your Tingler is called a *boli*. It's used in puppet shows as the puppet's singing voice. It's also used to provide rhythm in action scenes—the high squeaky sound can be heard even over the drums.

Water Gong

Try this experiment over the sink, in your bathtub, or in a wading pool on a hot summer day.

What Do I Need?

- pot lid that will hold water when it's upside down (a flat lid won't work)
- water
- carrot
- spoon
- pencil eraser
- stick

Ask a grown-up if you can borrow a pot lid to make a Water Gong.

What Do I Do?

1 Pick the lid up by the knob. Hold the lid upside down and run a little water into it. It doesn't matter how much. You need enough so that you can slosh it around without spilling it all out. In the lid for a 2-quart saucepan, we use about ¼ cup.

2 Use your carrot to tap once on the lid. Slosh the water around. You'll hear a ringing note that wavers and changes with the sloshing water.

3 Tap the lid on other spots and listen to how the sound changes. Try tapping with different things: your knuckles, a spoon, a pencil eraser, a stick. Each one may give you a different sound.

4 Get your Water Gong ringing and watch the water. Do you see ripples? Touch the lid lightly with your hand and you can feel the vibrations that make the water ripple and make the sound you hear.

5 If you feel like it (and if your parents say it's okay), try different pot lids. Find the ones that make the sounds you like best.

What's Going On?

Troubleshooting

If you don't get a good sound from your pot lid, make sure that you are holding the lid by the handle. If you hold it by the rim or touch any part of the metal, you may stop it from ringing. If you don't get a bell-like sound when you tap the rim of the lid, try tapping it in a different spot. If all else fails, try another pot lid. Some work better than others.

Why does the sound of the Water Gong change when you slosh the water?

When you tap your Water Gong with the carrot, you start it vibrating. Like the reed of the Straw Oboe, the metal vibrates with many different frequencies simultaneously. As these vibrations travel through the metal, some add together and sound louder. The size, shape, and thickness of the metal determine how the vibrations travel—and that helps determine which frequencies are loudest.

The metal under the pool of water in your Water Gong can't vibrate as freely as the metal elsewhere in the gong. When you swirl the water around, you are changing what parts of the metal can vibrate freely. Sometimes the moving water stops the high frequencies from vibrating, and at other times it stops the low frequencies. So the swirling water changes the note that you hear.

Awash in water music

When you thump on water-filled lids in your sink, you're part of a long tradition of water and music. Musicians in a variety of cultures have developed instruments that make use of the musical properties of water.

In North America, a number of Native American tribes played drums that were filled with water. The drum's tone could be adjusted by changing the level of the water. In West Africa, a water drum is made by floating a bowl-shaped section of dried gourd upside down in a pail of water. The musician (usually a woman) taps the floating gourd with a spoon or a stick. In India, musicians use bamboo sticks to play the *jaltarang*, a set of porcelain bowls filled with different amounts of water.

In Europe, fifteenth-century musicians played tuned glasses. Each glass contained a little water, and musicians played the glasses by wetting their fingers and stroking the rims to produce high, pure notes. (You can make a similar sound by wetting your finger and stroking the rim of a wineglass.) In the 1760s, American inventor Benjamin Franklin, intrigued by musical glasses, created an instrument called the *glass harmonica*. Glass bowls spun on a spindle, rotating through a trough of water that moistened their rims. The glass harmonica was very popular in its time—both Mozart and Beethoven composed for it—but subsequently the instrument fell out of favor.

CANdemonium

Recycle some cans to make a Bonko for great after-dinner music!

What Do I Need?

- tin cans (you'll need at least 3 cans of the same size)
- can opener
- sturdy tape (masking tape is okay, but plastic packing tape or duct tape works best)
- towel
- wooden spoon
- pencil

TIPS ON CANS

- Bonkos made from cans of different sizes will all sound different. Try making Bonkos from little cans (like soup), bigger cans (like dog food), or really big cans (like tomato juice or Hawaiian Punch). With a set of Bonkos, your whole family can make some interesting music together.
- You can plan ahead and save your cans as you use them. Or you can do what the Fowler family did—plan a special dinner of canned foods and create your Bonkos after you eat.
- Make sure that your cans have flat bottoms that you can cut off with a can opener. Cans with rounded bottoms won't work.

What Do I Do?

1 Ask a grown-up to use the can opener to cut off the bottoms of all of the cans—*except one.* Leave the bottom on that one. (If you're using different sizes of cans, make sure one can of each size has a bottom.)

2 Wash the insides of the cans and let them dry. (Be careful of the cut edges. They might be sharp.)

3 Take a can that still has a bottom and put it on the counter, open end up. Put another can of the same size on top of it. Tape them together.

4 Put the next can on top of the other two, and tape it to them. Now you have a Bonko that's three cans long, with one closed end and one open end. (You can also make a four- or five-can Bonko if you have enough cans.)

5 Put a towel down on your kitchen floor. Hold your Bonko open end up, and bonk it up and down on the towel. Try making different sounds. You can make your own rhythms by bonking faster or slower, softer or harder. If you hold your hand over the opening as you bonk, does that change the sound?

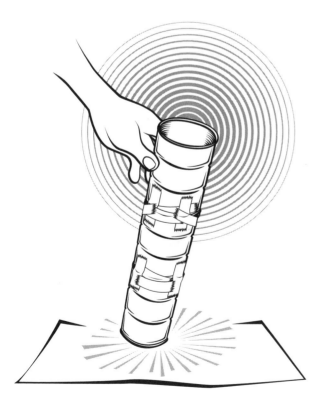

What's Going On?

Why does a long Bonko make a deeper sound than a short Bonko?

Compare two Bonkos that are made of cans of the same size. You'll find that the longer Bonko makes a lower-pitched sound than the shorter Bonko.

Rather than talking about pitch, scientists sometimes talk about a sound's *frequency*. Every sound begins with a vibration, and a sound's frequency is the rate of vibration—the number of times something vibrates in a unit of time. Something that's vibrating very fast—like the steam rushing out of a whistling teakettle or the metal of a tiny bell—makes a high-pitched, high-frequency sound. Something that's vibrating more slowly—like the drumhead of a bass drum or the metal of a big bell—makes a low-pitched, low-frequency sound.

When air inside a Bonko vibrates, it makes a sound that contains many different frequencies. This complex sound bounces around inside the metal tube. Sometimes vibrations of the same frequency overlap and add together. When that happens, sounds with that frequency get louder. The length of the Bonko helps determine which sounds get louder. Long Bonkos amplify low-frequency (low-pitched) sounds; short Bonkos amplify high-frequency (high-pitched) sounds.

An Orchestra in a Can

You can play your Bonko in a lot of different ways. Here are some of our favorites. Try coming up with others of your own!

Drums—Turn your Bonko upside down so the closed end is on top. Hit it with your hands like you'd play a conga drum or hit it with a wooden spoon for a louder sound.

Echo Tube—Sing, whistle, or talk into the open end of your Bonko and hear it echo. If you sing a scale into your Bonko, it will really vibrate with some notes and not as much with others. Put your hand gently on the closed end and you can *feel* it vibrate, too!

Washboard—Hold the Bonko open end up, and run a pencil up and down the *outside,* over the ridges of the cans. This is like a *guiro,* a Mexican instrument made from a carved gourd.

Astounding Sounds from All Around

Have you ever seen an instrument like the Bonko?

Maybe not in America. But all over the world—from Africa to South America—people use objects like your Bonko for dances and special ceremonies.

Some of these tubes are only about a foot long, but others are as tall as a grown-up man. People who study music call them all *stamping tubes.* Each culture has its own name for this instrument.

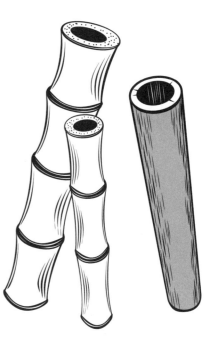

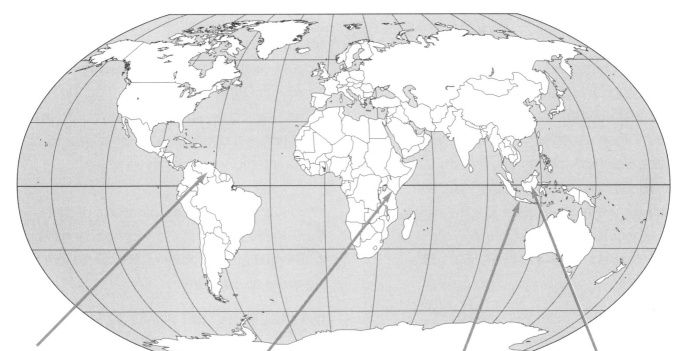

In Venezuela, they are called *quitiplas* and are made out of cane or hollow wood.

In Kenya and Tanzania, they are called *bazaras.* They are made out of bamboo, sometimes with slits cut in the sides. People pound them on the ground, but they also hit them with sticks to make a different sound.

In the islands of West Java, they are called *kendang awi.* These are made of bamboo, and two of them—one large, one small—are played together.

In Borneo, pieces of dried fruit are put into tubes of bamboo so that the tubes will also rattle when they hit the ground.

Playing with Rhythm

Use your new instruments to experiment with different rhythms.

The musical instruments that you've made aren't much good for playing familiar tunes like "Twinkle, Twinkle, Little Star" or "Happy Birthday to You." Those songs rely on melody, the arrangement of sounds of different pitches in a particular order. Your instruments aren't great for playing melodies, but they *are* great for experimenting with rhythm.

Try experimenting with these rhythm activities.

What Do I Need?

- Some rhythm instruments or other ways to make noises. If you don't have instruments, you can clap your hands, stamp your feet, or snap your fingers.
- A few people who want to experiment with rhythm.

FASCINATING RHYTHMS

This activity from R. Murray Schafer's book *Ear Cleaning* was designed to help music students practice their rhythmic skills.

What Do I Do?

1 Assign a different sound to each of the numbers 1, 2, and 3, and repeat that sound that number of times. For instance, 1 could be the sound of your Bonko, so you bonk your Bonko once; 2 could be the rattle of the Rain Stick, so you shake your Rain Stick twice; 3 could be stamping your foot, so you stamp your foot three times.

2 Now try all the combinations of these simple rhythms, moving from one group to the next as smoothly as you can. Here's the order to do them in:

123 132 231 213 321 312

3 If you can do the rhythms in step 2, try moving on to four variables, which would give you twenty-four different rhythmic combinations.

KEEP THE BEAT

This one's a little harder.

What Do I Do?

1 Tap a regular rhythm with your foot, accenting the first beat: **1,** 2, 3; **1,** 2, 3; **1,** 2, 3. Keep it going! Keep the beat slow and regular, and keep the accent on the first beat.

2 The beat you've established is called a *meter.* Now let's add a rhythm. Have your partner bonk the Bonko or shake the Rain Stick twice for every toe tap, like this:

Tap: **1** 2 3 **1** 2 3 **1** 2 3

Rhythm: xx xx xx xx xx xx xx xx xx

3 Have your partner change the rhythm of the Bonko or Rain Stick while you keep tapping your toe in the same steady meter.

4 Now have your partner use the Bonko or Rain Stick to beat out the words to this familiar song. If you like, you can sing along.

sing:	My	coun-try	tis	of thee
tap:	1	2	3	1	2	3
rhythm:	X	X	X	X	X	X

AFRICAN POLYRHYTHMS

If all that was easy, here's a challenge.

What Do I Do?

1 Take a look at the intricate rhythmic pattern shown below. This is a polyrhythm, which means it's made up of two different rhythms going on at the same time.

2 This particular polyrhythm is from the Ewe (Eh-way) people of Ghana. The first part of the pattern is intended for a bell and the second for a rattle, but you can substitute your Bonko and your Rain Stick—or you can clap or snap your fingers. First, try doing each pattern alone. Have one person count, while the other bonks the Bonko or shakes the Rain Stick.

3 After you can do each pattern alone, try putting put the patterns together. These two simple rhythms combine to produce a complicated rhythm. Good luck!

What Else Can I Do with Music?

If you liked experimenting with sound, try building some instruments of your own invention.

Oliver DiCicco is a member of a group of musical performance artists called Mobius Operandi. He builds musical instruments that aren't like anything you've ever seen.

Why would anyone build his own instruments rather than buy them in a store? Oliver says that he builds instruments because he wants to create his own kind of music, a kind of music that has never been heard before.

How does Oliver go about building a musical instrument? Sometimes he starts by thinking about an ordinary instrument and figuring out how he could change it and make something new. You could try doing that. How could you change your Bonko? Or your Straw Oboe?

At other times, Oliver starts by finding stuff that he wants to experiment with—like wood,

glass, or wires. You could experiment with stuff that you have around your house. Can you make a musical instrument out of an empty soda bottle? Blow across the top to make a hooting noise—or tap it to make a ringing noise. What happens if you put water in the bottle?

"I do a lot of experimenting," Oliver says. "What happens isn't always what you expect. Sometimes, when you're experimenting, you find happy accidents."

Try lots of different ways to make sounds and you'll find your own happy accidents!

The Exploratorium's Home Scientists have used their instruments on many occasions. The Eskimo students of Marshall School in Alaska used them during the annual end-of-the-year parade through their village. The Opotow-Chang family used their instruments as noisemakers during the Jewish holiday of Purim. Can you think of a special occasion when you can play your own unique music?

8

HEAR HERE!

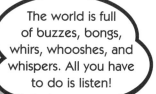

The world is full of buzzes, bongs, whirs, whooshes, and whispers. All you have to do is listen!

Suppose you're sitting in a classroom on a warm spring day. The teacher is talking, but you're thinking about what you're going to be doing after school. There are many sounds—birds are singing outside the window and people are walking down the hall—but you aren't paying attention to those sounds, any more than you are paying attention to what the teacher is saying.

Just then the teacher says your name. Suddenly you are jerked out of your daydream. You weren't really listening—but you heard your name. Your name is an important sound that catches your attention.

All around you, things are banging, whirring, squawking, rustling, buzzing, and making all kinds of sounds. Those sounds get into your ears and become signals that go to your brain. Your brain takes those signals and figures out whether you have to pay attention to a sound or not. You can ignore the birds outside the window, but you'd better pay attention when the teacher says your name!

Most people learn to tune out the world, ignoring most of the sounds they hear. But sometimes it's fun to listen to all the world's sounds—even the ones that most people think are unimportant. Brenda Hutchinson, a composer who sometimes builds exhibits at the Exploratorium, listens to everyday sounds as if they were music. She records common sounds and then uses her recordings to make her own uncommon music.

Brenda has helped the rest of the Exploratorium staff learn to listen to the world as she does. Now we all pay attention to sounds that everyone else ignores. Some of these are sounds that only one person at a time can hear—like the ringing of Secret Bells or the strumming of the Ear Guitar. Others are sounds that most people don't bother really listening to—like the rattling of the Cups of Mystery.

Pay attention to your ears, and you'll find yourself listening to the world in a whole new way.

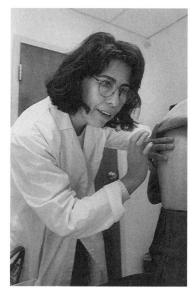

Sounds tell you about the world. A doctor thumps on your back to learn about what's inside you. If your lungs are full of air (as they should be), it makes a different sound than if your lungs contain some liquid (a sign that you're sick).

To find out if a melon is ripe, you can thump on it—just like a doctor thumps on your back. A ripe melon will have a different sound than one that's unripe.

Sound Safari

Even if you live in a quiet place, it's never really silent. You may be surprised by all the sounds around you!

What Do I Need?

- your hands
- your ears

What Do I Do?

1 Close your eyes. Be very quiet and listen for a few minutes. What sounds do you hear?

2 Cup your hands behind your ears and listen again. Do you hear different sounds? Are some sounds louder?

3 Cup your hands in front of your ears. What do you hear now? Walk around with your hands in different shapes around your ears and see if that changes the sounds that you hear.

4 Do you hear sounds from people? From animals? From machines? From water? What's the loudest sound you can hear? There are lots of ways you can talk about the sounds you hear.

- You can say what made the sound—"I hear the refrigerator door opening."
- You can say what the sound is like—"It sounds like a bell, very far away."
- You can use words like *buzz* or *tick-tock.* Those words imitate the sounds they describe. That's called *onomatopoeia* (pronounced "ahn-o-mat-o-pee-ah").

5 You can make your own onomatopoeia. Listen to the sounds around you and make up words for them. What's the sound a water balloon makes when it hits the sidewalk? How about cereal being poured into a bowl? Or a pair of sneakers going around in the dryer? If you want, you can draw pictures of your sound words, too.

POW! ZAP!

Comic book writers use onomatopoeia to make their stories seem more real. See if you can match these comic book sound words to the actions that go with them. It may be easier if you say the words out loud.

1. CHAKATA-CHAKATA-CHAKATA
2. SCRRTCH
3. THPLPLP!
4. FWOOSH!
5. SPLOOOOOSH!
6. EEEEEEEEERRRR
7. R-R-RURKK-K-K

A. Kid sticking out her tongue and making a raspberry.
B. Car running out of gas.
C. Superhero blowing out a fire.
D. Train going down the tracks.
E. Fire engine's siren.
F. Big guy jumping into a swimming pool.
G. Someone striking a match.

answers: 1-D; 2-G; 3-A; 4-C; 5-F; 6-E; 7-B

What's Going On?

Why bother trying the Sound Safari? After all, I'm always listening.

You're always listening, but if you're like most of us, you're not always paying attention. Most of us tend to shut out any repeated sound that carries no useful information. So we ignore some sounds and listen to others. All this filtering takes place subconsciously—unless you decide to tune in.

On the Sound Safari, you listen to all the sounds around you—even the ones that seem uninteresting or unimportant. Think about how you might describe each sound. Is it a continuous drone or does it start and stop? Is it high-pitched, like the whine of a washing machine on the spin cycle—or low-pitched, like the rumble of a dryer? Can you hum the pitch? Does the sound get louder or softer? Is it mostly a single pitch,

like the clear tone of a tuning fork, or is it a buzz, a mixture of many pitches?

Why bother? Because listening carefully may change how you feel about the sound you've chosen. John Cage, a noted twentieth-century composer who helped dissolve the barriers between musical and nonmusical sounds, suggested that people listen to the world with open ears, hearing all the sounds without judging and filtering them.

Next time you're standing at a busy street corner, listen—really listen—to the traffic. The cars rush by with a sibilant roar, not so different from the crash of the ocean surf. Yet many people consider the roar of the surf to be a beautiful sound—and most of us consider traffic noise a nuisance. Perhaps you, like John Cage, will come to love the sound of city traffic: "I love living on Sixth Avenue," he said of his New York home. "It has more sounds, and totally unpredictable sounds, than any place I've ever lived."

Head Harp

Make amazing sounds only *you* can hear!

What Do I Need?

- your hands
- your head
- a friend
- piece of string, about 5 feet long

What Do I Do?

1 Put your hands over your ears. Have your friend loop the string around your head, over your hands.

2 Pluck the string. You'll hear musical sounds, like someone plucking the strings of a giant harp.

3 Now let your friend have a turn. This time, you pluck the string that's looped around your friend's head. You won't hear much, but your friend will hear the secret music.

Wow! I Didn't Know That

After composer Ludwig van Beethoven went deaf, he could still hear his music by resting one end of a stick on the piano and holding the other end in his teeth. The sound traveled through the stick directly into the bones in his head to his inner ear. That's the same way the sound of the Head Harp gets to your ears!

Our Home Scientists discovered many interesting sounds. Bryan Patton liked the Head Harp because he thought it was "like being inside a violin." Matthew Smidebush said that rubbing the Head Harp string made it sound "like a jet taking off."

Secret Bells

An ordinary metal spoon can make astounding sounds!

What Do I Need?

- scissors
- string
- wire hanger
- table (or a wall, or a door)
- metal spoon

You can also try:

- fork
- potato peeler
- metal spatula (pancake flipper)
- cake rack

What Do I Do?

1 With your scissors, cut a piece of string about 3 feet long. (Grown-ups should cut a piece about 4 feet long.)

2 Hold the two ends of the string in one hand. The rest of the string will make a loop.

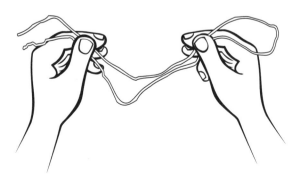

3 Lay the loop over the hook part of the hanger. Push the two ends through the loop, and pull them all the way through the other side. (This is easier to undo than a knot.)

4 Wrap the loose ends of the string two or three times around the first fingers on each hand.

5 Swing the hanger so it gently bumps against the leg of a table, or against a door. What did it sound like? Probably not much.

6 Now put your hands over the openings of your ears. (Don't put your fingers *in* your ears!) Hold your hands tight to the sides of your head. Lean over and gently bump the hanger again.

7 Wow! Now what does it sound like? Church bells? Chimes?

8 Want to hear what a spoon sounds like? Unwrap your fingers, then pull on the loop end of the string. The whole string will come off the hanger, and you can reloop it around the spoon.

Try this with other things from your kitchen.

What's Going On?

What's going on when I hear a sound?

You hear sounds when vibrations get inside your ears and stimulate your nerves to send electrical signals to your brain.

Suppose, for instance, that you are pounding on a drum. The drumhead starts vibrating. As the drumhead vibrates, it bumps into air molecules and starts them bouncing to and fro. Those bouncing air molecules bump into other air molecules and start them moving. This chain reaction of moving air molecules carries sound through the air in a series of pulsating pressure waves that we call *sound*.

Sound waves carry vibrations from the drum into your ears. Inside your ear, moving air molecules push on your eardrum and start it vibrating. Your eardrum, in turn, pushes on the bones of your middle ear, the tiniest bones in your body. These bones act like a set of levers, pushing against the thin membrane that covers the opening to your inner ear.

The movement of this membrane makes pressure waves in the fluid inside the cochlea, where cells with tiny sensing hairs transform the waves into electrical signals. These electrical signals travel along the auditory nerve to your brain. When

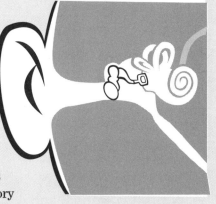

these electrical signals reach your brain, you hear a sound—the beat of a drum.

Why can you hear the music of the Head Harp only when the string is around your head? How do the Secret Bells work?

When you pluck on the string that's wrapped around your friend's head, the string starts vibrating. To reach your ears, the vibrations in the string must push on the air molecules to make sound waves that travel through the air. But the string isn't very large and it doesn't push on very many air molecules. So sound vibrations don't travel easily from the string into the air.

When the string is around your own head, the sound can take a more direct route to your ears. Rather than traveling through the air, the vibrations can travel through your hands and through the bone of your skull directly to the fluid inside your cochlea in your inner ear. Instead of traveling from solid to air and back to solid, the vibrations move from one solid (the string) to another (your bones), and then into the fluid of your cochlea. As a result, the sound you hear is much louder and richer.

The same thing happens with Secret Bells. When you put your hands over your ears, you provide a path that lets more of the vibrations reach your ears. When your hands aren't over your ears, you hear a faint, high-pitched, tinny sound. When you put your hands over your ears, you hear deep, resonant, bell-like tones. The hanger makes the same sound in both situations, but in one you provide a path that lets more of the sound reach your ears.

Ear Guitar

Share some secret sounds with a friend.

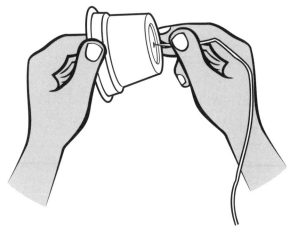

What Do I Need?

- nail (you'll also need a hammer if you use tin cans)
- two empty yogurt cups (you can also use two tin cans)
- scissors
- string
- bar of soap
- paper clips
- a friend

3 Wet the bar of soap. Rub one end of the string on the soap, then roll the string in your fingers so it's pointy. Poke the end of the string through the hole into the cup.

4 Reach into the cup with your fingers and pull the string a few inches. Tie the end of the string to a paper clip.

What Do I Do?

1 Use the nail to poke a hole in the center of the bottom of each yogurt cup. (If you use tin cans, have a grown-up make a hole with a hammer and the nail.)

2 With your scissors, cut a piece of string that's about 15 feet long.

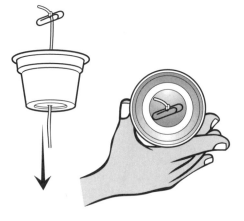

5 Do steps 3 and 4 again with the other cup and the other end of the string.

6 Now you've got an Ear Guitar! Hold one cup up to your ear, and give the other cup to your friend. Tell your friend to walk away from you until the string is tight, then hold his cup up to his own ear. When one of you plucks the string, both of you can hear the sound!

7 Is the sound you hear when you pluck the string different from the sound when your friend plucks the string? Does the sound change when the string is tighter or looser?

Tell-a-Cup

You can also use your Ear Guitar as a telephone! Have your friend walk away until the string is tight. Hold your cup up to your ear, and have your friend talk into her cup. Can you hear what she's saying?

What's Going On?

How does the Ear Guitar work?

When you pluck the string on an Ear Guitar, the string starts vibrating. The vibration in the string starts the bottom of the cup vibrating, which starts the air inside the cup vibrating. The cup helps channel those vibrating air molecules into your ear—so you hear the sound loud and clear.

Your voice, like other sounds, is a vibration. (Put your hand on your throat as you talk and you'll feel the vibrations.) When you talk into one of the cups, the vibrations of your voice travel into the cup, then from the cup into the string, and then back into the other cup. The cup channels your voice into your friend's ear.

Your yogurt-cup telephone works if the string between the two cups can vibrate freely. Pinch the string between the two cups, and your friend won't hear your voice as well. You may also discover that the string between the cups must be pulled tight, or your telephone won't work. If the string is loose, the sound vibrations die out before they reach the other cup.

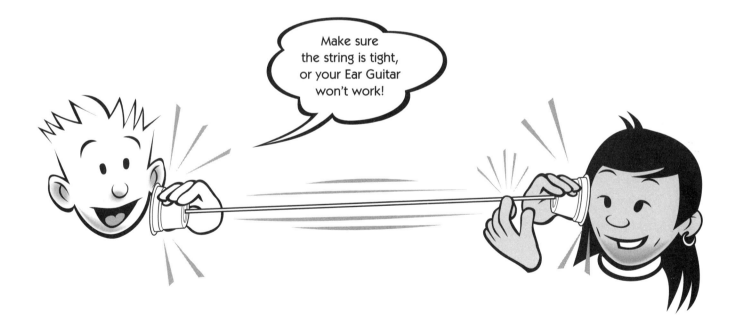

Make sure the string is tight, or your Ear Guitar won't work!

Cups of Mystery

Fool your friends! Who can guess what's in the Cups of Mystery?

What Do I Need?

- several friends (this is a good game to play at a party or with a lot of people)
- A lot of different small things. At the Exploratorium, we've used beans, rice, paper clips, pennies, corn flakes, salt, M&M's, plastic dinosaurs, macaroni, sand, and lots more. You can use anything you want.
- paper cups
- rubber bands
- marker
- aluminum foil (or paper towels)
- paper
- pencils (one for each person)

What Do I Do?

Before other people get to your house:

1 Gather up some small things. You can pick as many different things as you want. You'll need one paper cup and one rubber band for each thing.

2 Give each thing a number. With the marker, write a number on each cup. If corn flakes are 1, put some of them in the cup marked 1. Make an answer list and be sure that what's in each cup matches that same number on the list!

3 Cover each cup with aluminum foil or a piece of paper towel. Put a rubber band around the cup to keep the cover on.

4 Make another list with no numbers. Write down all the things that are in the cups—plus five or six things that aren't. Mix up the order, too. That'll give your friends some clues, but won't give the answers away. Put all the cups and the mixed-up list on a table. (And hide the answer list!)

When people get to your house:

5 Give each person paper and a pencil. Tell them they have to solve the mystery just by listening. They can shake the cups and look at the list on the table—but no fair peeking into the cups! Have everyone write down their guesses about what's inside each cup.

6 After 10 minutes, ask everyone to give their answers. Some cups may be tricky, and people will guess very different things. That's really fun! Look at your answer list and tell them what was really in each cup.

If you want to keep score, a person gets one point for each right answer. A good prize for the winner might be a toy elephant—for the person who had the best ears!

Robannie Smidebush, one of our Home Scientists, suggests that you put "yummy edible things" inside each cup. Whoever guesses right gets to eat (or share) what's in the cup. Do you know what gummy worms sound like? Heidi Schweizer, another Home Scientist, took Cups of Mystery to her kindergarten class for show-and-tell.

Listening to the Tube

Make your own sound effects using stuff from around your house.

Turn on your TV and close your eyes for a few minutes. What sounds do you hear?

When you're watching TV, you're also listening. You may hear people talking, and usually there's some music. If you listen carefully, you'll hear other sounds too—like a door closing or footsteps walking across a floor or the sound of thunder.

Most of those sounds were made in a studio by people called Foley artists. Movie microphones are set to pick up actor's voices, not other noises. So Foley artists watch a tape of a show and then use everyday things to make sounds that match what's happening on the screen. They experiment to find just the right sounds, and you can too!

What Do I Need?

- TV
- VCR
- some things that make interesting sounds (see the box on page 101 for some ideas)
- tape recorder (if you want)

What Do I Do?

1 In the box on page 101 are some sound effects tricks that Foley artists have used. Can you make those sounds with things you have around the house? Play around and see what other neat sounds you can make.

2 If you want to experiment with the work a real Foley artist does, you can try matching sounds to what you see on TV. Ask a grown-up to videotape your favorite TV show. While you play the tape, watch—and listen—very carefully. Pay attention to the sounds so you'll know what effects you need to create.

3 Try to find things around your house that will make those sounds. If you have a tape recorder, you may want to record your sound effects and play them back to hear how they sound. Keep experimenting until you get some effects you really like.

MAKE YOUR OWN SOUND EFFECTS

To make some sound effects, you don't need any props—all you need is your own body:

- Use your mouth to make the sound of wind or a train whistle or a bird's song.
- Pop your finger in your cheek to make the sound of a cork coming out of a bottle.
- For the sound of someone knocking on a door, rap your knuckles on the floor, a table—or on a real door.

Here are some other sound effects Foley artists have created:

Prop/Action	Sounds Like
rattling a cookie sheet	thunder
squeezing a box of cornstarch	someone walking through snow
shaking one dried bean inside a blown-up balloon	a bass drum
shaking one dried bean inside a paper envelope	a rattlesnake
a tube filled with nails and beans (like the Rain Stick on page 76)	rain
scrabbling your fingernails on a Frisbee	a dog walking across a kitchen floor
wetting your thumb and rubbing it on a blown-up balloon	a squeaky door opening
clopping half a coconut or a wooden salad bowl on the floor	a horse's hooves

4 Now play the videotape with the sound turned way down, just enough so you can hear the people talking. Use your Foley props to create the other sounds that go with the actions on the screen.

Wow! I Didn't Know That!

Most of the sounds that Foley artists create for TV and movies are different kinds of footsteps. An average Foley studio has fifteen feet of sidewalk, divided into squares. Each square is made from a different material—marble, sand, concrete, wood, gravel. A Foley artist may work with more than twenty pairs of shoes, to mimic the sounds of feet walking in anything from high heels to army boots.

What Else Can I Learn by Listening?

If you want to keep exploring and experimenting with listening, here are some things you can try.

The Shape of a Sound

Suppose you didn't want to use words—but you wanted to draw a sound on paper. Can you come up with a shape that matches a sound? Which of these shapes do you think looks like the howl of a wolf? Which one looks like an explosion?

Try to draw shapes that match the sounds sounds around you.

Close Your Eyes and Listen

If you see the Golden Gate Bridge, you know you're in San Francisco. Many cities and towns have landmarks—buildings or statues or monuments that everyone knows belong to that place. Many cities and towns also have sounds that belong to that place. In San Francisco, one of those sounds is the moaning of foghorns. Another is the clanging of cable car bells. Listen to the sounds where you live and try to find one that lets you know that you're home.

Submarine Sounds

Next time you're going for a swim, try listening underwater. Have someone talk to you when you're above the water, then have them keep talking when you go underwater. Can you still understand the words? Ask your friend to sing a song. When your ears are underwater, you may know the tune, but you probably can't understand the words. Plug your ears when you are underwater, and the sounds you hear will be just as loud as they were with your ears unplugged. When you're underwater, most of the sound you hear travels through the water to the bones of your skull, rather than through your ears.

MYSTERIOUS MIXTURES

> You can mix ordinary ingredients to make some really weird stuff!

At the Exploratorium, one of our most popular workshops is called Messy Science. People come and mix things together, fool around, and experiment. Sometimes, what they end up with isn't what they expect.

Other scientists have also made some very interesting discoveries that way. James Wright was an engineer at General Electric during World War II. His job was to create a cheap substitute for rubber. He experimented with a lot of different chemicals, and one day he mixed boric acid and silicone oil together.

Vivian Altmann runs the Exploratorium's Messy Science workshop, where people have great fun with goo!

The result was a stretchy goo that bounced better than rubber and didn't fall apart when it was very hot or very cold. It even did something rubber couldn't do—when it was squashed onto a page of newspaper comics, it picked up the ink from the pictures.

Unfortunately, there didn't seem to be any practical use for the goo. People fooled around with it for a couple of years, but even though it was interesting stuff, it was a failure as a rubber substitute.

But in 1945, an advertising writer named Paul Hodgson went to a party where someone was playing with James Wright's goo. Hodgson was a partner in a toy store, and he thought the goo looked like fun stuff. He bought a big mass of it for $147 and hired a college student to roll it into one-ounce balls. Hodgson sold each ball inside a plastic egg, and gave the goo a new name. He called it Silly Putty.

Silly Putty became an overnight sensation. Fifty years later, there is still no real practical use for the stuff, but it's one of the best-selling toys of all time.

In this chapter, you'll find some ways to make a few kinds of goo of your own. Fool around with them and see what happens. Your kitchen is a great place to experiment with mixing things together.

NOTHING ELSE IS Silly Putty
THE REAL SOLID LIQUID

James Wright, an engineer at General Electric, invented Silly Putty, a wonderful kind of goo.

Monster Mallows

In the microwave, an ordinary marshmallow will puff up until it's enormous!

What Do I Need?

- marshmallows
- paper plates or paper towels
- microwave oven
- toothpicks (if you want)
- food coloring (if you want)

What Do I Do?

1 Get a grown-up to help you.

2 Put two marshmallows on a paper plate (or a paper towel).

3 Put the plate in the microwave. Set the timer for 1 minute (60 seconds) on High.

4 Stand back and watch through the window of the microwave. After about 20 seconds, you'll see the marshmallows start to puff up. They'll get to about four times their original size!

5 When the microwave turns off, take the plate out and put it on the counter.

6 Wait a few seconds, then pull one marshmallow off. (Be careful, it may be hot.) The bottom may stick to the plate or paper towel. Is the marshmallow hollow inside? Is the inside the same color as the outside? When you eat it, is it soft or crunchy?

7 Leave the other marsh-mallow on the plate and watch it for a minute. When it shrinks back down, you can pull it with your fingers. Make it into whatever shape you want. It will stay in that shape and get hard and crunchy. You can eat it, too.

8 Try microwaving another marshmallow for 1½ minutes (90 seconds). Does it get bigger than the first one? What color is the inside?

Expand-a-Face

Dip a toothpick into food coloring and draw a face on your marshmallow—before you put it in the microwave. As the marshmallow puffs up, the face will get bigger and bigger.

Wow! I Didn't Know That!

Ancient Egyptians made a puffy white treat out of honey and the dried, carrot-shaped root of the marsh mallow plant, which grows in fields and swamps. Today we still call these candies *marshmallows,* but now they're made with sugar and gelatin. Marsh mallow root is still used to make some kinds of glue.

DON'T microwave a marshmallow for more than 2 minutes. It will just turn dark brown and make a stinky, sticky mess.

What's Going On?

Why do marshmallows puff up in the microwave?

Marshmallows are mostly sugar and water wrapped around a bunch of air bubbles. When you cook marshmallows in your microwave oven, several things happen at once. The microwaves make the water molecules vibrate very quickly—which makes the water heat up. The hot water warms the sugar, which softens a little. The hot water also warms the air bubbles.

When you warm air in a closed container, the gas molecules move around faster and push harder against the walls of the container. As the air in the bubbles warms up, the air molecules bounce around faster and faster and push harder against the bubble walls. Since the sugar walls are warm and soft, the bubbles expand, and the marshmallow puffs up. If it puffs up too much, some air bubbles burst, and the marshmallow deflates like a popped balloon.

When you take the marshmallow out of the microwave and it cools off, the bubbles shrink and the sugar hardens again. When the microwaved marshmallow cools, it's dry and crunchy. We think that's because some of the water in the marshmallow evaporates when the marshmallow is hot.

If you cook your marshmallow for too long, it turns brown or black inside. That happens when the sugar gets so hot that it starts to burn.

Tips for parents

In the springtime, it's fun to expand marshmallow chicks and bunnies instead of regular marshmallows.

Soap Drops Derby
You can make a liquid kaleidoscope!

What Do I Need?

- milk (only whole or 2% will work)
- newspapers
- a shallow container or dish
- food coloring
- dishwashing soap
- a saucer or a plastic lid
- toothpicks
- cotton swabs (if you want)
- rubbing alcohol (if you want)

2 Put a piece of newspaper somewhere flat—on a table or your kitchen counter—and put your dish on top of it. Pour about ½ inch of milk into the dish.

3 Let the milk sit for a minute or two.

4 Put one drop of food coloring into the dish, near the side. Put a few different-colored drops in a pattern around the dish.

5 Watch the drops. They may grow a little bigger, but they probably won't move around much.

6 Pour some dishwashing soap onto your saucer or lid. Dip the end of a toothpick into the dish soap, then touch it to the center of the milk. Wow! What happened? All the colors scooted to the sides of the dish!

What Do I Do?

1 Take the milk out of the refrigerator a half hour before you want to try this. Soap Drops Derby works best at room temperature.

7 Dip the toothpick into the soap again, and touch it to a blob of color. Does the color move? Do the colors on the other side of the dish move?

8 Rub dishwashing soap over the bottom half of a food coloring bottle. Stand the bottle in the middle of the dish. Watch the colors swirl and stream around it. They'll swirl for a few minutes.

9 You can keep dipping the toothpick in soap and touching it to the colors to make them move for about 20 minutes.

Turbo Colors

For fast-action colors, make another bowl of milk with food coloring drops. Dip a cotton swab in rubbing alcohol and touch it to the surface of the milk. Super swirls! Now dip it in the rubbing alcohol again and touch it to a blob of color. Wow!

What's Going On?

What makes the milk in Soap Drops Derby move like that?

Have you ever taken a close look at a drop of water on a shiny leaf or a newly waxed car? (If you haven't, put a drop of water on a piece of waxed paper and take a look at it now.) On a waxy surface, a water drop doesn't lie flat like a puddle. Instead it looks more like a tiny water balloon. The drop seems to be contained by a stretchy membrane; this phenomenon is known as *surface tension*. If you add a touch of soap to a water drop, it flattens like a burst water balloon. Soap reduces the surface tension of the water, and gravity pulls the drop flat.

Water acts like it has a stretchy skin because water molecules are strongly attracted to each other; they tend to stick together. Soap molecules squeeze between the water molecules, pushing them apart and reducing the water's surface tension.

What does all this have to do with Soap Drops Derby? Milk, which is mostly water, also has surface tension. When you touch the surface of the milk with a drop of soap, you reduce the surface tension of the milk at that spot. Since the surface tension of the milk at the soapy spot is much weaker than it is in the rest of the milk, the water molecules elsewhere in the bowl pull water molecules away from the soapy spot. The movement of the food coloring reveals these currents in the milk.

Water acts like it has a stretchy skin on its surface. That's why a water strider can skate on the surface of a still pond without getting its feet wet.

ExploraGoo

With a grown-up's help, you can make this weird, wiggly stuff right in your own kitchen!

What Do I Need?

- newspaper
- plastic wrap or waxed paper
- one 4-ounce bottle of white glue
- two large plastic containers or glass bowls
- measuring cup
- water
- food coloring (if you want)
- measuring spoon (teaspoon)
- Boraxo powdered hand soap or a box of borax (in the laundry aisle of most supermarkets)
- cookie cutters (if you want)
- small plastic container with a lid (margarine or cream cheese tubs are perfect)

What Do I Do?

1 This is really, really messy stuff. Put some newspaper on your kitchen counter or table. Then cover the newspaper with plastic wrap. (ExploraGoo sticks to paper.)

2 Pour the bottle of glue into one bowl. Add ½ cup of water and some food coloring. (Our favorite color is 10 drops of yellow and 5 drops of green.) Mix everything together.

3 In the other bowl, put 2 teaspoons of Boraxo powdered soap (or 1 teaspoon of borax powder). Add ½ cup of water and stir until the borax is dissolved. (You may still see a few specks of the soap. That's okay.)

4 Pour the colored glue-water mixture slowly into the borax-water mixture. A big glob of ExploraGoo will form right before your eyes!

5 Reach into the bowl with both hands and pick up the glob. It will be very, very, very slippery. Pick up as much as you can. (There will be a little water and some pieces of goo left in the bottom of the bowl. That's okay.)

6 ExploraGoo will get less slippery the more you play with it. Let it slide back and forth from one hand to the other for a few minutes. (If it's too much for your hands to hold, give half to a friend to play with.)

If you put it down, make sure it is on the plastic wrap, *not* the paper. Don't put it on carpet or furniture or clothes, either. It's really sticky stuff.

Don't put ExploraGoo in your mouth. It tastes yucky and it isn't good to eat.

Now What Do I Do?

- Can you stretch your ExploraGoo?
- It looks solid, but can you "pour" it from one hand to the other?
- If you pull it apart quickly, what happens?
- Can you pull off a piece and bounce it?
- If you press it into a yogurt container, does it make rude noises?
- Add a drop of food color to your ExploraGoo after you've played with it for a while. Play with it some more to make cool swirls of color.

Wow! I Didn't Know That!

Borax is a white crystal that is used in laundry soap, paint, pottery glazes, leather tanning, and in medicine. Most of the world's borax is mined in California—in Death Valley and the Mojave Desert—and in Tibet.

ExploraForms

Make a ball of ExploraGoo about the size of a small tangerine. Put it on a piece of plastic wrap. The ball will flatten out to a thin pancake. Leave it for an hour or two. Then cut out shapes with cookie cutters or scissors. (If the shapes still melt back to blobs, let the ExploraGoo dry out for another hour.) You can play with the shapes for an afternoon before they start to dry out and get crunchy. (*Don't* put the shapes back into the container with the rest of your ExploraGoo.)

What's Going On?

Don't let your child eat the ExploraGoo

The ingredients in ExploraGoo aren't poisonous, but they aren't food products either. Kids who eat paste and Play-doh may be tempted to eat their ExploraGoo. Don't let them. We haven't experimented to learn what will happen to a child who eats ExploraGoo, and we'd rather you didn't, either.

What is this ExploraGoo?

When you mixed up your ExploraGoo, you started a chemical reaction. The glue molecules and the borax molecules reacted with each other and combined to make a tangled structure of long, flexible, cross-linked chains. This structure—a giant molecule made up of thousands of smaller molecules—is called a *polymer*. Nylon and plastic are both polymers, much like your ExploraGoo.

Make a blob of ExploraGoo into a ball and try bouncing it. ExploraGoo (like rubber balls, car tires, and rubber bands) is bouncy because it's *elastic*. That means the ExploraGoo changes shape under pressure, but then returns to its original form. Elasticity is what gives a ball its bounce—the ball flattens out when it

hits the ground, then springs back to its original shape. When the ball returns to its original shape, it pushes off the ground and bounces back.

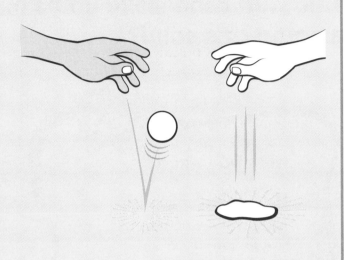

The long, tangled polymers that make up ExploraGoo (and rubber and many plastics) are called *elastomers*. Elastomers are what make these compounds so bouncy. When a blob made up of tangled polymers is put under pressure, the tangles straighten out temporarily. When the pressure is released, the molecules return to their tangles—and the blob bounces back.

Don't eat
your goo.
It's bad for you.

Outrageous Ooze

This stuff can't make up its mind—is it a liquid or a solid?

What Do I Need?

- newspaper
- measuring cups
- 1 cup of dry cornstarch
- large bowl or pan
- food coloring (if you want)
- ½ cup of water

3 Keep adding water until the Ooze feels like a liquid when you're mixing it slowly. Then try tapping on the surface with your finger or a spoon. When Ooze is just right, it won't splash—it will feel solid. If your Ooze is too powdery, add a little more water. If it's too wet, add more cornstarch.

4 Play around with your Ooze.

What Do I Do?

1 Put newspaper down on your counter or table.

2 Put the cornstarch into the bowl. Add a drop or two of food coloring. (Use whatever colors you like.) Add water slowly, mixing the cornstarch and water with your fingers until all the powder is wet.

- Pick up a handful and squeeze it. Stop squeezing and it will drip through your fingers.

- Rest your fingers on the surface of the Ooze. Let them sink down to the bottom of the bowl. Then try to pull them out fast. What happens?
- Take a blob and roll it between your hands to make a ball. Then stop rolling. The Ooze will trickle away between your fingers.
- Put a small plastic toy on the surface. Does it stay there or does it sink?

What's Going On?

Why does my Ooze act like that?

Your Ooze is made up of tiny, solid particles of cornstarch suspended in water. Chemists call this type of mixture a *colloid*.

As you found out when you experimented with your Ooze, this colloid behaves strangely. When you bang on it with a spoon or quickly squeeze a handful of Ooze, it freezes in place, acting like a solid. The harder you push, the thicker the Ooze becomes. But when you open your hand and let your Ooze ooze, it drips like a liquid. Try to stir the Ooze quickly with a finger, and it will resist your movement. Stir it slowly, and it will flow around your finger easily.

Smack water with a spoon and it splashes.

Smack Ooze with a spoon and it acts like a solid.

Most liquids don't act like that. If you stir a cup of water with your finger, the water moves out of the way easily—and it doesn't matter whether you stir quickly or slowly. Your finger is applying what a physicist would call a *sideways shearing force* to the water. In response, the water *shears*, or moves out of the way. The behavior of your Ooze relates to its *viscosity*, or resistance to flow. Water's viscosity doesn't change when you apply a shearing force—but the viscosity of your Ooze does.

Back in the 1700s, Isaac Newton identified the properties of an ideal liquid. Water and other liquids that have the properties that Newton identified are called *Newtonian fluids*. Your Ooze doesn't act like Newton's ideal fluid. It's a *non-Newtonian fluid*.

There are many non-Newtonian fluids around. They don't all behave like your Ooze, but each one is weird in its own way. Ketchup, for example, is a non-Newtonian fluid. (The scientific term for this type of non-Newtonian fluid is *thixotropic*. That comes from the Greek words *thixis*, which means "the act of handling," and *trope*, meaning "change.")

Quicksand is a non-Newtonian fluid that acts more like your Ooze—it gets more viscous when you apply a shearing force. If you ever find yourself sinking in a pool of quicksand (or a vat of cornstarch and water), try swimming toward the shore very slowly. The slower you move, the less the quicksand or cornstarch will resist your movement.

What Else Can I Mix Together?

Some foods do amazing things when you mix them together.

Color-Changing Cabbage Juice

Get a jar of pickled red cabbage at the grocery store. Drain some of the red juice into two bowls.

Add baking soda to the first bowl. The liquid will fizz, and it will also change color!

After you've watched it fizz, pour vinegar into the same bowl. The liquid will change color again, and fizz even more. You'll see two different-colored layers of fizz.

Cabbage juice is an indicator. If you add an acid (like vinegar) to the juice, it turns pink. If you add a base (like baking soda), the cabbage juice turns blue.

If you want more cabbage juice, ask a grown-up to chop up a head of red cabbage and put it in a pot of water. Let it soak for a couple of hours, then drain the red liquid into a jar. Keep your jar of cabbage juice in the refrigerator for future experiments.

More Cabbage Experiments

Put some cabbage juice in two or three small bowls so you can do a couple of different experiments.

- What can you add to the cabbage juice to make it turn blue? What's in your kitchen that acts like baking soda? Will baking powder work? How about other white powders, like flour or powdered sugar?
- What can you add to the cabbage juice to make it turn red? What's in your kitchen that tastes sour like vinegar? Will lemon juice work? How about orange juice, or sour cream?
- If you add something that turned the cabbage juice blue to something that turned it red, does that mixture fizz? (For more on fizzing mixtures, see "Balloon Blow-up" on page 4.)

When I added baking soda, the cabbage juice fizzed. That's because it was *pickled* cabbage, and it already had vinegar in it.

114

Encouraging Kids to Keep Exploring

Linda Shore

We hope that this book has helped you and your kids to start exploring the world in a new way. But now that you finished this book, you may be wondering how you can keep your child's interest in science going.

The truth is, it's much easier than you think.

Children are born doing science. By randomly touching objects and placing things in their mouths, toddlers learn what is hot or cold, sweet or sour, sharp or dull, rough or smooth. Preschoolers learn almost everything scientifically—through trial and error. For older children, daily life is full of scientific discovery. Combing the cat's hair can be a lesson in static charge. Watching toys sink and float in the bathtub is a chance to investigate the principle of buoyancy. By playing catch, kids make discoveries about gravity and trajectories. By building towers out of blocks, they explore principles of size, scale, and basic engineering. Kids learn about the world by experimenting and observing—trying things out and watching what happens. That's science.

Of course, kids don't always come up with the same explanations for electricity, buoyancy, or gravity that a scientist would under the same circumstances. Although children create logical explanations based on what they experience, their ideas about the world are often at odds with scientific laws and theories. But by retaining their curiosity and continuing their observations, over the years children might put together the scientific explanation for themselves.

We all start life so full of curiosity, eager to experiment and explore. Science—the observation and investigation of the world—is a natural part of our lives. Unfortunately, on the way to adulthood, most kids seem to lose touch with their interest in science.

Why does this happen? Experts say that the change seems to start in junior high school, when science is often presented as a list of facts and formulas to memorize. Instead of a natural exploration, science suddenly becomes difficult and dull. Added to this are the stereotypical images in movies and on TV that depict scientists as weird, nerdy-looking guys in white lab coats. Faced with these images of science and scientists, few teenagers decide science is fun and something they want to do when they grow up.

But some kids manage to retain their scientific curiosity into adulthood. Why do some of us choose scientific careers despite our school experiences and media stereotypes? And how can grown-ups help children retain their curiosity and interest in figuring out how the world works? While I was listening to Jane Goodall lecture on her life and famous studies of chimpanzees, an answer came to me.

Jane Goodall began her lecture by telling the audience of her earliest studies of animal behavior. She was five years old when she became curious

about the chickens in the henhouse. How did the chickens make eggs? Where exactly did the eggs come from? To answer her questions, Jane did what any good scientist would do. She decided to hide quietly in the corner of the barn and observe. She spent all night in the hay watching the chickens—waiting for them to do whatever they did to make eggs. Finally, after waiting and watching all night long, Jane saw it happen—and her mystery was solved.

Even though the barn was dirty and cold, Jane's parents didn't discourage their daughter's explorations. Jane wasn't ordered back into the warm, clean house. She wasn't asked to return to the comfort of her bed. Instead, Jane's natural curiosity about life in the henhouse was allowed to play itself out. Jane's parents gave her permission to be a scientist.

At about the same time as her chicken observations, Jane also became curious about the earthworms in the garden. Jane gathered all the worms she could find and took them to her bedroom. She laid the slimy, writhing creatures on her bed. Jane examined the worms and noted subtle differences in size, shape, color, and texture. She observed how they moved.

I could only imagine what my mother's reaction would have been to this experiment! But Jane Goodall described how supportive her mother had been when she discovered the nature study in progress. Jane's mother reminded her that the worms would die if they weren't returned to the soil. She asked Jane to put the worms back in the garden as soon as she was through.

Jane Goodall never lost her childhood curiosity about animals and animal behavior. She acknowledged that if her mother had discouraged her first studies of animals, she might not have chosen a scientific career and ultimately would never have performed her landmark studies of chimpanzee behavior. I came to the conclusion that parental involvement and encouragement must be a key factor in a child's retaining scientific curiosity past puberty. Many experts believe this too.

What can you do to nurture a child's curiosity about the world? How can you be more like Jane Goodall's mother? The answer is simple: continue to encourage children to act on their natural curiosity and participate as much as you can.

Like many grown-ups, you might be frightened of science. The thought of helping a kid with a science experiment may make you uncomfortable. Perhaps you think you don't know enough science and you're afraid you "won't get the right answer" without the help of a book like this one. Relax. The way to find the "right answer" is to explore and experiment. Besides, sometimes no one knows the right answer—not even scientists.

Of course, it is unrealistic to expect every child to grow up to be Jane Goodall. But with your encouragement, your child may grow up appreciating what science is and what scientists do. More important, your child will also learn something about problem solving and logical thinking—important skills for all kids, regardless of what they choose to be when they grow up. And who knows—you might even rediscover the child science explorer inside yourself.

Suggested Reading

If you'd like to keep on exploring, here are some books that can help you.

Books for Kids Ages 7 to 9

1. Blowing, Bouncing, Bursting Bubbles
Soap Science by J. L. Bell (New York: Addison-Wesley, 1993). Activities and explanations about soap bubbles, soap films, and soap making.

Bubbles by Bernie Zubrowski (Boston: Little, Brown and Co., 1979). A good introduction to soap bubbles, bubble films, and blowing bubbles.

2. It's Colorific!
Eyewitness Art: Color (New York: Dorling Kindersley, 1993). Great full-color illustrations explain color and how it is used in all types of art.

3. Seeing the Light
Eyewitness Science: Light by David Burni (New York: Dorling Kindersley, 1992). Informative and beautifully illustrated with full-color photos of light and lenses.

Bending Light by Pat Murphy and the Exploratorium Staff (Boston: Little, Brown and Co., 1993). Dozens of hands-on activities for exploring light and lenses from one of the authors of this book.

4. Seeing Isn't Believing
How to Make Optical Illusion Tricks & Toys by E. Richard Churchill (New York: Sterling Publishing Co., 1989). Explanations for many kinds of optical illusions and instructions for creating some illusions of your own.

5. Rings, Wings, and Other Flying Things
The Visual Dictionary of Flight (New York: Dorling Kindersley, 1992). Full-color photos and lively text cover a wide range of different flying things.

6. Dramatic Static
Eyewitness Science: Electricity by Steve Parker (New York: Dorling Kindersley, 1992). Full-color photos illustrate the story of electricity from static and lightning to motors and power plants.

The Usborne Young Scientist: Electricity by Philip Chapman (London: Usborne Publishing, Ltd., 1976, 1991). A good introduction to electricity from atoms and lightning through batteries, currents, and motors.

7. Marvelous Music and Astounding Sounds
The World of Music by Nicola Barber and Mary Mure (Parsippany, N.J.: Silver Burdett Press, 1995). A look at international musical instruments—strings, winds, percussion. Includes discussions of music, pitch, rhythm, and melody as well, all illustrated with full-color drawings and photos.

8. Hear Here!
The Listening Book: Discovering Your Own Music by W. A. Mathieu. (Boston: Shambhala Publications, 1991). This is a great book for anyone who has ears. A guide to help you rediscover the sounds around you.

9. Mysterious Mixtures
Usborne Pocket Scientist Chemistry Experiments by Mary Johnson. (London: Usborne Publishing, Ltd., 1981, 1988). Fun experiments with soap, baking soda, vinegar, and other household ingredients, with simple explanations about what's going on.

Simple Kitchen Experiments: Learning Science with Everyday Foods by Muriel Mandel (New York: Sterling Publishing Co., 1994). Dozens of experiments you can do in your own kitchen.

Books for Older Kids and Grown-ups without a Science Background

The Cartoon Guide to Physics, by Larry Gonick and Art Huffman. (New York: Harper Perennial, 1990). A playful, yet accurate cartoon approach to physics.

The Cheshire Cat and Other Eye-Popping Experiments on How We See the World by Paul Doherty, Don Rathjen, and the Exploratorium Teacher Institute (New York: John Wiley and Sons, 1991, 1995). Instructions for building miniature versions of two dozen of the Exploratorium's exhibits on vision and perception.

Drumming at the Edge of Magic: A Journey into the Spirit of Percussion by Mickey Hart with Jay Stevens (New York: HarperCollins, 1990). A history and exploration of drums and other percussion instruments around the world by the former drummer for the Grateful Dead. A companion music CD is also available.

Girls and Young Women Inventing, by Frances A. Karnes and Suzanne M. Bean (Minneapolis: Free Spirit Publishing, 1995). This book presents an inspiring description of girls and women who invent.

How in the World, by Reader's Digest (Pleasantville, N.Y.: Reader's Digest Association, Inc., 1990). A comprehensive book that answers commonly asked questions in science.

How Science Works: 100 Ways Parents and Kids Can Share the Secrets of Science by Judith Hahn (Pleasantville, N.Y.: Reader's Digest Association, Inc., 1991). A great family guide to major science topics, including light, sound, energy, chemistry, and electricity, all illustrated with diagrams and full-color photos.

The Magic Wand and Other Experiments on Light and Color by Paul Doherty, Don Rathjen, and the Exploratorium Teacher Institute (New York: John Wiley and Sons, 1991, 1995). Instructions for building miniature versions of two dozen of the Exploratorium's exhibits on light and color.

Physics for Kids: 49 Easy Experiments with Acoustics by Robert W. Wood (Blue Ridge Summit, Penn.: TAB Books, 1991). Experiments with sound, sound waves, and hearing.

Return to the Fold by John M. Collins, Don Garwood, and Thay Yang (New York: McGraw-Hill, Inc., 1995). The man who holds the world's record for the longest paper airplane flight explains how to design and make your own paper aircraft.

The Usborne Illustrated Dictionary Series (London: Usborne Publishing, Ltd.): *The Dictionary of Biology,* by C. Stockley (1986); *Dictionary of Physics,* by C. Oxlade, C. Stokley, and J. Wertheim (1986); and *Dictionary of Chemistry,* by J. Wertheim, C. Oxlade, J. Waterhouse (1986). Beautifully illustrated and clearly written, these books provide explanations of basic science concepts.

The Visual Dictionary of the Human Body (New York: Dorling Kindersley, 1991) and *The Visual Dictionary of Physics* by Jack Challoner (New York: Dorling Kindersley, 1995). Using vivid photographs and illustrations, these books provide a basic understanding of human anatomy and physics.

The Way Things Work by David Macaulay (Boston: Houghton Mifflin Co., 1988). A visual encyclopedia that dissects a variety of everyday objects to show how they work.

Advanced Books for Grown-ups with a Background in Science

Light and Color in the Outdoors by M.G.J. Minnaert (New York: Springer Verlag, 1954). A classic source of information on optics in the outdoors.

Perception by Irvin Rock (New York: Scientific American Books, 1984). A thorough and readable book about visual perception and illusions.

Seeing the Light by David Falk, Dieter Brill, and David Stork (New York: John Wiley and Sons, 1986). A very readable textbook on optics and vision.

Many of these books are available from the Exploratorium Store at the museum, where you can shop in person or order by phone at 1-415-561-0393.

Thank You Very Much!

At the Exploratorium, no one works alone. The Science-at-Home team had the help and support of many people—inside the Exploratorium and out. These experiments and activities came from years of work and play by the staff and teachers at the School in the Exploratorium, the Exploratorium Teachers' Institute, and the Exploratorium's Children's Outreach Program. Many people on the Exploratorium staff helped us by telling us about their favorite activities, testing those activities, or reviewing what we wrote. We'd especially like to thank Vivian Altmann, Debra Coy Bainum, Ruth Brown, Paul Doherty, Ken Finn, Cappy Greene, Tien Huynh-Dinh, Roni Locati, Eric Muller, and Mark Nichol.

We also want to thank those who helped us turn a bunch of words into a book. Jason Gorski not only drew the characters, his illustrations helped us find the clearest way to present the information. Mark McGowan, Randy Comer, Stephanie Syjuco, and Emaline Mann-Sanchez designed the original graphic format for the material, and Lucy Albanese and Kelly Soong worked with us to redesign the material in book form.

The Exploratorium has many friends who helped us find the right overall shape and direction for the book. Thanks to Phil Morrison, Phylis Morrison, Jenefer Merrill, and Bernie Zubrowski for their thoughtful advice. Thanks to David Sobel for his editing acumen and patience.

This book would not have been possible without the moral and administrative support of many people. Thanks to Kurt Feichtmeir for being the keeper of the budget (a thankless but necessary task), and for remaining cheerful through it all. Thanks to Mary Beth Williams for her tireless work on mailings, databases, and analysis of question-naires. Thanks to Megan Bury for her assistance in the final hour. And thanks to Dominique Langlois, Rob Semper, and Goèry Delacôte for giving us the institutional backing we needed.

And finally, most important of all, thanks to the Informal Science Education Program of the National Science Foundation and the Pacific Telesis Founda-tion. Without funding provided by these institutions, the testing and development that made this book what it is would not have been possible. Special thanks to our NSF program officer, Roger Mitchell, for his advice, patience, and understanding.

And Thank You Even More!

Hundreds of families across America (and a few in other countries) tested these activities and provided us with their comments and ideas. This book would not have been possible without them! We would like to thank the following families for being pioneering Home Scientists.

These families tested ten Science-at-Home packets for us:

Adams family
Beckman family
Berenson family
Vicki Gordon family
Gould family
Harpster family
Hitchner family
Kim family
O'Brien family
Shaff family
Stahl family
Swain family

These families tested nine Science-at-Home packets for us:

Barton family
Fisher family
Heid family
Landis family
Lee family
Stevenson family
Torphammer family

These families tested eight Science-at-Home packets for us:

Barry family
Delaney family
Dunn family

Justin Feldman family
Foote family
Kincaid family
Nilsson family
Cindy Sandoval family

These families tested seven Science-at-Home packets for us:

Cifor family
Chesbro family
Feyer-Cohen family
Graff family
Judd-Clear family
Rodriguez-Warner family
Rosano family
Rowe-Willisson family
SooHoo family
Tennyson family
Van De Boom family
Walter-Bowman family

These families tested six Science-at-Home packets for us:

Bainum family
Beltrami family
Faneuf family
Frost family
Hinze family
Jaeger-Wolf family
Kelly-Shaw family
Liroff family
Manley family
Morris family
Rock-Lieberman family
Schachter-Lerner family
Smidebush family
Steinke family
Wolitzky family

These families tested five Science-at-Home packets for us:

Ajello family
Austin family
Belles family
Briggs family
Brown family
Cole-Hardenbergh family
Failor family
Finnegan family
Grumann family
Gumkowski family
Hairston family
Miriam Morgan family
Muskett family
Pogash-Wood family
Shannon-Kromer family
Stone family
Struttman family
Tsang family
Vavra family
Wanerus-Hughes family
Weisman-Farber family
Camille Wright family
Zagar family

These families tested four Science-at-Home packets for us:

Blair-Stolk family
Burns family
Cahill family
Chapman family
Creed family
Danforth family
Dickson family
Fowler family
Hartley-Guider family
Hollister family
Kaneko-Jones family
Kenton Parker family
Lewenstein family
Perez family
Pettifer family

Popka family
Rockwood family
Sakamoto family
Schweizer family
Kip Smith family
Paige Smith family
Troiano family
Woodbury family

These families tested three
Science-at-Home packets for us:

Abelson-Kish family
Alahan family
Beigel family
Bicheler family
Black family
Buesseler family
Carlson-Hartzell family
D'Este family
Day family
English-Ricker family
Gano family
Gertsch family
Haskett family
Kahn family
Kelani family
Kolonkowsky family
Lau family
Lum family
Millar family
Nunes family
Rosner family
Setnan family
Reed Smith family
Wang family
Werner family
Wildegrube family

These families tested two
Science-at-Home packets for us:

Banks family
Bien family
Bingham family
Burke-Lazarus family
Carey family
Cleeves family
Council family
Cram family
Duckert-Casner family

Fenchel-Vernon family
Froemelt family
Grooms family
Hendrickson family
Heydet family
Ho family
Holm-Nielsen family
Howie family
Hunt family
Katherine and Bob Jones family
Kathail family
Krebs-Ridgway family
Lekach-House family
Lemme family
Lowder family
McCormick family
McLeish family
Medrano family
Morton family
Murray family
Nelson family
Newby family
Opotow-Chang family
Orton family
Painter-Heston family
Martha Parker family
Pera family
Phelan family
Ptak family
Risken family
Rivkin-Haas family
Robinson family
Rosen family
Russ family
Salin family
Sargent-Wineman family
Schreyer family
Smolens-Burchfield family
Spruill family
Marty Stern family
Strom family
Crystal Sullivan family
Taniguchi family
Tarlin family
Mrs.Torbett's class
Towle family
Townsend family
Toy-Early family
Trabosh-Schmitz family
Uhrich family

Van der Loos family
Visser family
Wamsley family
Wickstrom family
Wienands family
Yokoyama family
Zeitvogel family

These families tested one
Science-at-Home packet for us:

Aitel-Jurow family
Akmese-Schwab family
Allison-Keim family
Anderson family
Arnold-Hoff family
Auclair family
Babcock family
Bacon family
Baron-Porter family
Beaupre family
Bell family
Berman family
Bernstein family
Berwick-Gaer family
Bon family
Braunstein family
Bridges family
Brown family
Burkhardt family
Campbell family
Caver family
Mario Chang family
Chung family
Clayton family
Cooper-Colby family
Cruz family
Davis family
Degener family
Dermody family
Dudek family
Dudziak family
Fall family
Federman family
Leonard Feldman family
Felton family
Finer-Broselow family
Debra Fischer family
Florin family
Frain family

Fuerst family
Gee family
Gilbert family
Gary Gordon family
Gottlieb family
Granger family
Green family
Grimstad family
Gruner family
Guillaume family
Hall family
Hamscher family
Hawkinson family
Hazen-Knuepfel family
Hileman family
Hino family
Hodges family
Holley family
Hooker family
Howarter family
Hunter family
James family
Jaquysh family
Jeffries family
Gary Jones family
Kelley family
Kintzer family
Kissinger family
Koffel-Yu family
Kositsky-Haimen family
Kowalczykowski family
Kubin family
LaCava family
Lauer family
Leslie-Murphy family
Lien family
Linstadt family
Lippman family
Lohr family
Long Marris family
Lowe family

Lozoff family
Luna family
Lynphi family
Magas family
Manakawa family
Maravelius family
Marinelli family
McAlister family
McCormack family
McDonald family
McEwen family
McIntyre family
Mikalonis family
Miranker family
Montgomery family
Morais family
Pat Morgan family
Sara Morgan family
Morrow family
Muller family
Munekawa family
Ng family
Nielson family
Nixon family
Nunez family
Pankow family
Patton family
Pepmiller family
Perrigo family
Phi family
Pinkham family
Pistritto family
Ravano family
Reder family
Richeda family
Rosenbluth family
Rubin family
Sandoe family
Carmen Sandoval family
Sanford family
Santos family

Schnurr family
Scholtz family
Scott family
Seaman family
Shaft family
Shah family
Shue family
Sinicropi-Yao family
Sleeper family
Smyth family
Sneeringer family
Stansfield family
Nadine Stern family
Steyer-Taylor family
Rob Sullivan family
Swansburg family
Terman-Frydenlund family
Terwilliger family
Thomason family
Thompson family
Tuufuli family
Van Hecke family
Volgers family
Wagstaff family
Welohr family
Wilkerson family
Lisa Williams family
Witham family
Wolf family
Wood family
Mike Wright family
Eric Wright family
Zaleski family
Wolf family
Wood family
Mike Wright family
Eric Wright family
Yokoyama family
Zaleski family

Index